Conflict Management Training Activities

by

Don L. Sorenson, Ph.D.

**Promoting Cooperative Learning
and Conflict Resolution
in Middle and High Schools**

Copyright 1994
Educational Media Corporation®

ISBN 0-932796-65-6
Library of Congress Catalog No. 94-070678
Printing (Last Digit)
9   8   7   6   5   4   3   2

Publisher—

Educational Media Corporation®
PO Box 21311
Minneapolis, MN 55421-0311
(612) 781-0088

Graphic design—

Earl Sorenson

Artwork—

Reid Sorenson

Dedication

To my sons, *Mark, Daren,* and *Brent* who taught me much about managing conflicts with their marvelous abilities to handle their dad in stressful situations and...

To my wife, *Arlene,* who has guided me to gentler approaches for handling life's conflicts.

Acknowledgments

From all of us who use experiential training activities in working with others, we give thanks to the hundreds of people who have developed and refined these activities through the years. While it is often difficult to trace an activity to its originator, there are several who deserve special credit for their contributions to this field:

J. William Pfeifer and *John E. Jones*, University Associates, La Jolla, California for their work in developing structured activities for groups;

David W. Johnson and *Roger T. Johnson*, University of Minnesota, Minneapolis, for their work in developing cooperative learning and conflict management strategies;

Robert D. Myrick and *Joe Wittmer*, University of Florida, Gainesville, for their work in developing the facilitative model for use in teacher education and peer helping; and

Richard Bandler and *John Grinder* for developing Neuro Linguistic Programming, a model of human communication and behavior which makes it possible to describe any activity in a detailed way that allows us to make therapeutic changes efficiently.

Educational Media Corporation®, Box 21311, Minneapolis, MN 55421-0311

Table of Contents

Introduction 7
1   Getting Acquainted 11
2   Breaking Boundaries 14
3   Rating Yourself and Others 17
4   Meeting Basic Needs 20
5   Depending on Others 23
6   Giving Instructions 25
7   Following Directions 27
8   Working as a Group 30
9   Solving Problems Collectively 32
10   Choosing New Colors 36
11   Getting Everyone Involved 40
12   Dividing Discs, Desserts, and Deserves 47
13   Seeing Isn't Always Believing 51
14   Mapping Our Worlds 59
15   Sharing Our Maps 61
16   Eyeing the Eyes 64
17   Retrieving Missing Pieces 67
18   Entertaining Conflicts 73
19   Journaling Your Conflicts 76
20   Standing on Your Values 78
21   Brainstorming 81
22   Handling Put-Downs 83
23   Busting Balloons 86
24   Fighting Presumptions 88
25   Experiencing Conflicts 90
26   Sharing the Wealth 96
27   Splitting the Take 98
28   Drafting New Players 100
29   Exploring Negotiating Styles 103

30 Empowering the Beasts 108
31 Building Six-Inch Squares 114
32 Taking Note 118
33 Listening for Dollars 120
34 Attending to the Message 122
35 Misunderstanding Others and Being Misunderstood 124
36 Developing a Feeling Word Vocabulary 127
37 Finding Feeling Words 130
38 Listening and Responding 133
39 Questioning Questions 136
40 Trashing Pet Peeves 138
41 Giving and Receiving Feedback 140
42 Sharing Feelings and Perceptions 143
43 Unraveling the Situation 145
44 Generating Conflict Scenarios 147
45 Defining the Conflict 150
46 Mediating a Conflict 153
47 Planning a Day Out 156
Selected References 158

Educational Media Corporation®, Box 21311, Minneapolis, MN 55421-0311

Introduction

Conflict Management and Cooperative Learning

Are you concerned about the growing amounts of violence, fighting, namecalling, and other inappropriate methods your middle and high school students are using to handle conflicts? Would you like to take some specific steps to build a more peaceful and safe environment in which to work with them?

Conflicts are a part of our every day lives. By learning to manage them effectively, your students will be able to cope more effectively. When they learn the skills of effective *conflict management*, disputes that used to disrupt the learning environment and threaten the security and safety of everyone will definitely lessen in frequency and intensity.

By encouraging your students to take a more cooperative or win/win approach to learning and problem solving, you will find that your classroom will become more productive and peaceful.

Cooperative learning is a term that is applied to a structured program where students are assigned to groups to work together to solve problems and to master the material being studied. For cooperative learning to be effective, students need to become skillful in communicating, trusting, and working with others.

Any activity that develops communication, trust building, and leadership skills is appropriate in both conflict management and cooperative learning programs. By implementing the concepts taught through the training activities in this book, you and your students will learn to work together more effectively which will allow you to direct more energy and effort to the business of learning.

Pleasant and Unpleasant Conflicts

We learn and grow from conflicts—they are a necessary part of our learning experiences. However, conflicts can and do take a toll on us. We can all benefit by learning more effective ways of managing conflicts—learning how to resolve certain conflicts that would otherwise consume our energies and detract from our enjoyment.

It would be a dull life without conflicts. While we often think of conflicts as things that cause pain and distress, we welcome the opportunity to participate in certain conflicts like sports contests because we find joy in winning. We feel good about ourselves because we mastered the conflict—we won the contest.

But what about the losers, how do they feel? Do you remember how you felt the last time you lost a game of checkers, a softball game, or a race? You probably experienced some unpleasant feelings, but those feelings led you to resolve to do better—to practice and practice so that you could experience the pleasant feelings of winning next time.

Competition vs. Cooperation

We do a pretty good job of teaching *competition* in our schools and society. Everywhere we turn competition is encouraged—competition to win in sports, competition for the highest grades in class, and competition for the attention and affection of those who are important in our lives.

However, many tasks can be accomplished better by *cooperation*— not competition. Cooperation and competition are different styles of learning and functioning, and we need to know the differences between them. Much of what we learn about competition often contaminates our understanding of cooperation. Some of the concepts we apply to competitive learning are not appropriate in a cooperative learning situation.

One of these that is appropriate for competitive learning and not appropriate in the cooperative learning setting is the win/lose concept. When we engage in cooperative learning, it is no longer appropriate to think in terms of winning or losing. Everyone wins! We work together to accomplish the goal. We all grow and no one loses.

When we seek to improve the learning environment by reducing conflicts among students, we are seeking to change their perceptions that human interactions always require that someone be a winner and the other a loser. We are seeking to establish an environment of cooperation—to change the idea that we must constantly be in conflict with one another.

Causes of Conflicts

Sometimes when there are shortages of certain resources such as time, space, money, power, influence, and position, conflicts result. We get impatient with others when our time is limited and we have a task to accomplish. Prime real estate is in great demand as the prices reflect. There can be only one national champion in any given sport, and only one person can be President of the United States at a time.

Conflicts also result because we are not all the same. Each of us creates our own internal map or model of the world. Our behavior, thoughts, and feelings are based on the models we have created. Therefore, we have different ways of perceiving the world, different assumptions, different values, and different ways of expressing ourselves.

When we find ourselves in conflict with another, we can learn a great deal by being willing to explore the differences between ourselves that led to the conflict.

Educational Media Corporation®, Box 21311, Minneapolis, MN 55421-0311

It is not necessary that we resolve all conflicts and eliminate our differences. However, a peaceful society requires that we learn to explore and express our differences in positive ways. We should learn to celebrate the similarities we discover and to acknowledge and respect our diversities. Then we can explore ways of working together to meet each other's needs while continuing to respect our different feelings, values, and perceptions.

Positive and Negative Approaches to Conflicts

Although we tend to respond to conflicts in a variety of ways depending on the situation, we generally have a characteristic style we employ when we face conflicts.

We may choose to *avoid* the conflict entirely, cutting off the relationship when we find ourselves in conflict. We may *deny* that a conflict even exists. Denial is another method of responding to conflicts.

An opposite method of approaching conflicts is with *aggression*. When we adapt an aggressive manner of handling conflicts, we attack or blame others. We push for our points of view, ignoring the attitudes and feelings of others. We believe we are right and others are always wrong.

Avoidance, denial, and aggression are *not* positive ways of approaching conflicts. In a conflict management program, we seek to lessen the number of times negative approaches are used and increase the use of positive approaches.

Conflicts can and should be handled in a positive manner. Positive approaches permit us to grow from conflicts, learning new and better ways to respond and improving our interpersonal relationships with others. We learn more about others—and ourselves—by approaching conflicts positively.

How do we change a conflict situation from negative to positive? When we change from a competitive mind set to a cooperative one, we change from a win/lose mentality to a problem-solving approach.

Problem solving is based on the idea that we both can win—we both can emerge from the situation with the knowledge that our feelings were heard and respected and that our individual needs were addressed. While we may not become friends, we will gain a greater understanding of one another when we switch from perceiving the situation as a win/lose proposition to perceiving it as a mutual problem to be resolved.

Defining the Problem

How a problem is defined has a great deal to do with being able to find a mutually acceptable solution. Strong feelings may cloud the issue. It is necessary for us to listen carefully to each other, to restate what is being said, and to continue the process until the underlying issue has been resolved.

Skill and practice are required to be able to find the core of the problem in a conflict and to arrive at a solution that is acceptable to both. Your students can learn these skills and become effective partners in building a more cooperative learning climate by serving as student or peer mediators. A detailed presentation of the conflict resolution and mediation model for middle and high school students is presented in *Conflict Resolution and Mediation for Peer Helpers* (Sorenson, 1992).

However, skills alone are not sufficient. To be effective in the mediator and problem-solver roles, we must become aware of how we handle our own conflicts. We must become more aware of ourselves. Knowing ourselves is a prerequisite to helping others to know themselves.

About this Program

The activities that follow were chosen to provide the basis of a conflict management training program for middle and high school students. This program can be used in a classroom to teach conflict management and cooperative learning strategies or it can be the foundation for a peer mediator training program.

We begin with getting acquainted, trust building, and boundary breaking activities to establish a cooperative learning environment. We explore how we operate from our own unique internal models of the world which sometimes results in conflicts due to differences in perceptions and misunderstandings. Then we proceed to some activities where different characteristics of conflicts are explored. We conclude with activities to build skills in communication, problem solving, and conflict resolution.

The activities presented are not meant to be an all-inclusive program. They are designed to provide a jumping-off point and to stimulate your own creativity. Wherever possible, *reproducible* masters are provided of the materials and handouts needed to implement the activity.

Our sincerest best wishes go with you as you undertake the exciting adventure of promoting a more peaceful and productive learning environment in your school.

Educational Media Corporation®, Box 21311, Minneapolis, MN 55421-0311

Activity 1
Getting Acquainted

Introduction:

Before any group can function together, there must be a certain amount of trust. When we share something about ourselves with others, we take a risk.

Once we share something, the consequences of sharing it are out of our control. Whatever the receivers do with the information is up to them. They can either use what we have shared to help us or to hurt us.

If they use the information to help us grow and meet our needs, it will feel good.

If they use it to hurt us, it will hurt a great deal. The hurt will be greater than any positive feelings that might have resulted. So, why trust and share?

We have to believe that there will be many more times when people use what they know about us in a positive way than there will be times when people seek to hurt us. We trust and we share because we believe the *quantity* of positive experiences outweighs the few negative ones that we will experience.

It is wise, however, to begin a new group by taking low-level risks—sharing information that is relatively safe.

Purpose:

* To begin the process of working together
* To experience minimal risk-taking through disclosure

Materials:

* One copy of the Getting Acquainted Questionnaire for each participant, nametags, pencils or pens

Time:

- 15 minutes, plus time to process the activity

Procedure:

1. Prior to this activity you will have selected the participants for this program and explained your goals to the group. These activities can be used to encourage a cooperative learning atmosphere in your classroom, to teach conflict management skills, or to provide a foundation for a peer mediator program.
2. Distribute a copy of the Getting Acquainted Questionnaire to each participant. Instruct them to move about the room and obtain a signature on each of the lines. Set a time limit.
3. Each person can sign only one line on an individual's form.
4. Call time and discuss the activity.

Processing the Activity:

1. Which questions were easiest to find people to sign?
2. Were there any questions that you were reluctant to ask of others? Which questions?
3. What do we mean by low-risk and high-risk disclosures? Give examples of each.
4. Which person surprised you the most?
5. What did it feel like to share this type of information with others?
6. What questions would you suggest adding to the questionnaire?

Notes About this Activity:

_____
_____
_____
_____
_____
_____
_____

Educational Media Corporation®, Box 21311, Minneapolis, MN 55421-0311

Getting Acquainted Questionnaire

Who. . .

1. Has lived in a state that begins with M? _____

2. Is the youngest in the family? _____

3. Works part-time after school? _____

4. Has a unique pet? _____

5. Collects rare items? _____

6. Has lived in this city less than a year? _____

7. Doesn't like sports? _____

8. Lives in a yellow house? _____

9. Is the oldest in the family? _____

10. Is allergic to something? _____

11. Doesn't watch TV? _____

12. Has acted in a professional production? _____

13. Traveled to Europe last summer? _____

14. Owns stock in a company? _____

15. Sleeps in a bunk bed? _____

16. Has a savings account? _____

17. Has visited a jail or prison? _____

18. Was hospitalized for an illness or accident? _____

19. Has not flown in an airplane? _____

20. Has been on a cruise ship? _____

21. Can't swim? _____

22. Has a computer at home? _____

23. Doesn't like to play video games? _____

24. Has parents who are divorced or separated? _____

25. Has more than four brothers and sisters? _____

Activity 2
Breaking Boundaries

Introduction:

Building group cohesion requires that we get to know more about the others in the group—how they think, feel, and act in certain situations.

We can learn a lot about others simply by listening to how they respond to everyday questions. Some will be very willing to self-disclose a great deal about themselves while others will be very closed, often responding in a joking or humorous manner.

Purpose:

- To learn to listen to others and to form impressions based on their verbal responses
- To become more aware of others
- To remove barriers to relationships

Materials:

- Chairs in a circle

Time:

- 40 minutes

Procedure:

1. Have the group sit in a circle.
2. Tell them this activity is designed to permit them to get to know each other better. They are to listen to the responses of each person and to form some general impressions as the activity progresses. If they cannot think of a response, they may pass the first round. Everyone must respond to each question before proceeding to the next question. It is okay to have the same response as someone else in the group.
3. Go around and ask each question. Repeat the answers to reinforce the responses. Do not comment on the statements made by the members of the group.
4. Permit no discussion of the responses until the close of the activity.

Educational Media Corporation®, Box 21311, Minneapolis, MN 55421-0311

Questions

1. Which sport is your favorite?
2. What is the best movie you have ever seen?
3. What is your favorite color?
4. What is the title of the last book you have read?
5. What is the greatest offense one person could inflict on another?
6. What is your favorite TV show?
7. What feeling or emotion is strongest within you?
8. What do you want to be doing in five years?
9. What qualities do you prefer in your friends?
10. If you could travel anywhere, where would you choose to go first?
11. When do you feel the most lonely?
12. What person has had the greatest influence on your personality?
13. What is your biggest concern or worry?
14. What makes you feel the most secure?
15. If the end of the world was coming in ten minutes, what would you do in those last minutes?
16. For what would you give up your life?
17. If you could be something other than a human, what would you be?
18. What do you think people like in you the *most*?
19. What do you think people like in you the *least*?
20. What embarrasses you the most?
21. What do you love or cherish the most?
22. If you could live over one particular day in your life, what day would it be?

Processing the Activity:

Ask the group to answer the following questions in a go-around based on the impressions they formed from the answers to the first questions.

1. Which person did you learn the most about today?
2. Which person do you think you could get along with best?
3. Which person do you think was the least revealing today?
4. Which person do you think was the most honest?
5. Which person do you think is the most sensitive?
6. Which person would you like to learn more about?
7. Which person do you think enjoys life the most?
8. Which answer surprised you the most?
9. Which areas do you find the hardest to talk about?
10. Which answer from another person pleased you the most?

Notes About this Activity:

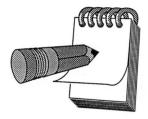

_____

_____

_____

_____

_____

_____

_____

Educational Media Corporation®, Box 21311, Minneapolis, MN 55421-0311

Activity 3
Rating Yourself and Others

Introduction:

We behave in certain ways depending on how we see ourselves. Our self-concept determines our behavior. We perceive the world through our self-concept. Self-concepts are learned and can be changed. They are influenced by how others see us. How others see us is not always the same as the way we see ourselves.

Purpose:

- To demonstrate that we generally evaluate ourselves as being above average

Materials:

- Two copies of the Self-Concept Rating Scale for each participant, pencils

Time:

- 15 minutes

Procedure:

1. Distribute one copy of the Self-Concept Rating Scale to each participant. Ask them to rate themselves on each characteristic using a five-point scale. Remind them that the midpoint (3) on the scale is to represent "average."

2. Collect the sheets and appoint someone to tally the results and calculate the mean (average). Engage the group in another activity or discussion while the tallies are made.

4. Later in the period, distribute a second rating sheet. This time, ask the group to rate the typical person in the group on the same five-point scale. Remind them that the midpoint on the scale (3) is to represent "average."

5. Collect these sheets and tally them. Calculate the mean (average score) on each characteristic. Display the results.

Processing the Activity:

1. Which mean set of scores would you predict would be higher (the self-evaluation or the evaluation of the average group member)?
2. Why do we tend to view ourselves as above the average?
3. How can average be average if all of the individuals in the group evaluate themselves as above average?
4. What are some of the feelings connected with being seen as average or below?
5. What are some of the advantages of perceiving ourselves as above average? What are some of the disadvantages?

Notes About this Activity:

_____

_____

_____

_____

_____

_____

_____

Educational Media Corporation®, Box 21311, Minneapolis, MN 55421-0311

Self-Concept Rating Scale

Positive Personality Characteristics

Please rate yourself on the following characteristics:

	Below Average		Average		Above Average
Honest	1	2	3	4	5
Open	1	2	3	4	5
Responsible	1	2	3	4	5
Trustworthy	1	2	3	4	5
Courageous	1	2	3	4	5
Courteous	1	2	3	4	5
Dependable	1	2	3	4	5
Genuine	1	2	3	4	5

Copy
✂
& Cut

Self-Concept Rating Scale

Positive Personality Characteristics

Please rate the typical person in your group on the following characteristics:

	Below Average		Average		Above Average
Honest	1	2	3	4	5
Open	1	2	3	4	5
Responsible	1	2	3	4	5
Trustworthy	1	2	3	4	5
Courageous	1	2	3	4	5
Courteous	1	2	3	4	5
Dependable	1	2	3	4	5
Genuine	1	2	3	4	5

Activity 4
Meeting Basic Needs

Introduction:

We all have basic needs. When these needs are not satisfied, we do not function well. When these needs are satisfied, our relationships with others and our productivity are enhanced.

Our most obvious needs are those of food, water, elimination, sleep, and shelter. These human needs are necessary in daily living and we often take them for granted. To these needs we might add the following *psychological* needs which also have been identified as essential:

- The need to be loved and accepted
- The need for security
- The need to belong
- The need to be independent, to take responsibility, and to make choices

Purpose:

- To focus on the things we do to meet the psychological needs of those persons close to us

Materials:

- A copy of the Basic Needs Worksheet for each participant, pencils

Time:

- 20 minutes, plus time to process the activity

Procedure:

1. Review our basic psychological needs, stressing that we function better when these needs are met.
2. Distribute copies of the Basic Needs Worksheet to all participants.
3. Working independently, the participants should give examples of specific things they do to meet the basic psychological needs of those who are important in their lives.

Processing the Activity:

1. Divide into small groups and discuss the various answers provided in the blanks.
2. List for the larger group any unique suggestions obtained from this exercise.

Notes About this Activity:

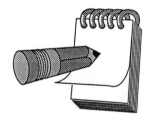

_____

_____

_____

_____

_____

_____

_____

Basic Needs Worksheet

1. For each of the following groups of people, give an example of something you have done to meet each of the following needs:

	The need to be loved and accepected	The need for security	The need to belong	The need to be independent, to take responsibility and to make choices
Parents				
Friends				
Siblings				
Classmates				
Teachers				

2. How would you behave to show respect to:

A. A new student? _____

_____

_____

B. Someone who does not speak the same language? _____

_____

_____

C. Someone has been put down by others? _____

_____

_____

Educational Media Corporation®, Box 21311, Minneapolis, MN 55421-0311

Activity 5

Depending on Others

Introduction:

Some things we can do alone, but many things require the cooperation of another. We can practice serving a tennis ball alone, but to play a game we need a partner. Much of what we do in life requires participating with others—working together. When we work or play alone, we are demonstrating our *in*dependence. When we cooperate with another, we are demonstrating *inter*dependence. When we work or play together, we are dependent upon each other to achieve an end result.

Purpose:

- To focus on the importance of cooperating with others
- To assess our preferences to work alone or with others

Materials:

- A copy of the Independent/Interdependent Worksheet for each participant

Time:

- 15 minutes, plus time to process the activity

Procedure:

1. Have each participant complete the Independent/Interdependent Worksheet independently.
2. Divide into small discussion groups to share responses.

Processing the Activity:

1. Were you surprised at the number of things that require the cooperation of others?
2. Looking at the ten things you like to do, do you prefer to spend your free time alone or with others?
3. What can you do to improve your relationships with others?

Independent/Interdependent Worksheet

1. Which of the following are easiest to do alone (A), which require interactions with others (O)?

A   O   1.   Get married

A   O   2.   Run 500 meters

A   O   3.   Skate

A   O   4.   Play hockey

A   O   5.   Bench press twice your weight

A   O   6.   Tutor mathematics

A   O   7.   Kick a ball

A   O   8.   Score a touchdown

A   O   9.   Argue

A   O   10.   Study

A   O   11.   March in a parade

A   O   12.   Ski downhill

A   O   13.   Pilot a jet

A   O   14.   Sing in a choir

A   O   15.   Play catch

A   O   16.   Read a book

2. List 10 things you like to do. Then, after you have listed the 10, check whether you prefer to do each activity alone (A) or with others (O).

A   O   1.   _____

A   O   2.   _____

A   O   3.   _____

A   O   4.   _____

A   O   5.   _____

A   O   6.   _____

A   O   7.   _____

A   O   8.   _____

A   O   9.   _____

A   O   10.   _____

3. Name three things you like to do by yourself:

1. _____

2. _____

3. _____

4. If you have some free time, would you rather spend it:

___ with others?

___ alone?

Educational Media Corporation®, Box 21311, Minneapolis, MN 55421-0311

Activity 6
Giving Instructions

Introduction:

Sometimes we must perform tasks under handicapping conditions. In these cases the assistance of others is both appreciated and necessary.

Working together is easier when communication flows freely both ways. However, sometimes we are in a position where we must follow the leadership of others without any opportunity to question or to ask for clarifications. Under these conditions our listening skills are very important.

Learning how to tune in to others and to follow instructions are very important skills. Equally important is the ability to give clear and concise instructions that can be followed easily.

Purpose:

- To demonstrate problems that can occur in one-way communication
- To develop strategies for communicating instructions clearly

Materials:

- Legos, Tinkertoys, or some items to be assembled
- Model to be assembled, blindfolds

Time:

- 20 minutes

Procedure:

1. Remind the group that there are some things that we cannot do alone. When working under a handicap, cooperation requires clear communication to solve a problem or to complete a task.
2. Introduce the concept of one-way communication and the importance of being a good listener when you cannot ask questions.
3. You may do this activity in pairs or you may have one "instructor" for the entire group.
4. If you choose, pair up the group around small tables. Give each pair some materials to assemble, (e.g., Tinkertoys, Legos).
5. Blindfold one partner. When the blindfold is in place, give the partner that is not blindfolded instructions on what to build. You might pre-assemble the item and take a picture of it or draw it on a sheet of paper.
6. Inform the teams that the exercise will be timed. When instructed to begin, the seeing partners instruct their blindfolded partners on what to build. The seeing partner cannot touch the materials; they are to describe the project and serve as eyes for their partners.
7. If the group is working in pairs, switch roles and repeat the exercise so everyone has a chance to assemble an object while blindfolded.

Processing the Activity:

1. What made it difficult to construct the object?
2. What assumptions did the seeing partner make about the process that needed to be changed?
3. How did it feel to be handicapped?
4. What frustrated you about your partner's instructions?
5. What specific instructions given made the project easier?
6. How does being able to ask questions facilitate communication?
7. What questions did you want to ask but couldn't?
8. Under what conditions are one-way communications effective?
9. How did it feel to be dependent upon another? (Remember, the seeing partner was also dependent upon the other partner to do the constructing.)

Notes About this Activity:

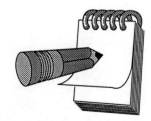

Educational Media Corporation®, Box 21311, Minneapolis, MN 55421-0311

Activity 7
Following Directions

Introduction:

When we work cooperatively with others, often we are required to follow the lead or instructions of those in positions of leadership. In today's fast-paced world, we are bombarded with a great deal of information which sometimes competes with other information for our attention. Problems result when we do not pay attention to instructions. Successful problem solving often requires that we read and follow instructions carefully.

Purpose:

- To demonstrate the importance of following instructions
- To illustrate that even the simplest instructions can be ignored

Materials:

- A copy of the Mathematics Quiz for each participant, pencils

Time:

- 10 minutes

Procedure:

1. Inform the group that this is a test of their mathematical abilities. It is a simple test involving easy addition, subtraction, multiplication, and division.

2. Distribute the Mathematics Quiz face down. Tell them not to turn them over until you say go.

3. Say, "When I say go, turn your papers over and work as fast as you can. As soon as you finish, turn your papers over and raise your hand. Ready, Go!"

4. Give your instructions in a hurry and do not allow any time for questions. Tell them time is short and they must work fast.

5. After 30 to 40 seconds have passed, interrupt the test and say, "I see most of you are finished. Let's check our answers."

6. Say, "The answer to number one, of course, is what?" Several will respond with 10. *Acknowledge* that 10 is correct. One or two will give the *correct* answer of 24.

7. Say, "Okay, the answer to number two to is what?" After two or three responses, note that there are different answers. Ask if they are all taking the same test? Then, ask the group to read the directions again *carefully*.

Processing the Activity:

1. How many did not read the directions? Why not?

2. How important are clearly understood directions to completing a task?

3. What happens when directions are not followed?

4. What assumptions were made that were in error? What affect did those assumptions have on being able to do the task?

5. What does the saying, "Haste makes waste," mean?

Notes About this Activity:

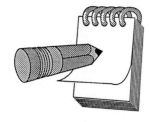

_____

_____

_____

_____

_____

_____

Educational Media Corporation®, Box 21311, Minneapolis, MN 55421-0311

Mathematics Quiz

Directions: In the following simple arithmetic problems, a plus (+) sign means to multiply, a divide (/) sign means to add, a minus (-) sign means to divide, and a times (x) sign means to subtract. Complete the problems following these directions.

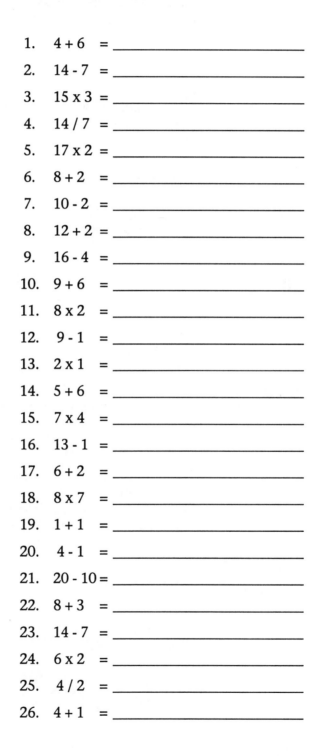

1. 4 + 6   = _____
2. 14 - 7 = _____
3. 15 x 3 = _____
4. 14 / 7 = _____
5. 17 x 2 = _____
6. 8 + 2   = _____
7. 10 - 2 = _____
8. 12 + 2 = _____
9. 16 - 4 = _____
10. 9 + 6   = _____
11. 8 x 2   = _____
12. 9 - 1   = _____
13. 2 x 1   = _____
14. 5 + 6   = _____
15. 7 x 4   = _____
16. 13 - 1 = _____
17. 6 + 2   = _____
18. 8 x 7   = _____
19. 1 + 1   = _____
20. 4 - 1   = _____
21. 20 - 10 = _____
22. 8 + 3   = _____
23. 14 - 7 = _____
24. 6 x 2   = _____
25. 4 / 2   = _____
26. 4 + 1   = _____

Activity 8
Working as a Group

Introduction:

Groups are important. Belonging to effective groups greatly increases the quality of our lives. Our personal identities are derived from the way in which we are perceived and treated by other members of the groups to which we belong.

Many of our goals can be achieved only with the cooperation of others. We pool our resources in groups to accomplish common objectives. Through the tasks below, we will experience some of the dynamics of a group as we work to achieve common goals.

Purpose:

- To experience the dynamics of a task-oriented group

Materials:

- Dependent upon the task selected

Procedure:

1. Divide the larger group into smaller groups. Select a task for each group from the following list and provide the required materials.

2. Appoint one person to serve as an observer. This person is to observe the contributions made by the other members of the group to accomplishing the group task. Observers should be prepared to comment on the group interaction at the close of the exercise.

Tasks:

1. Devise a game to be played with a large wad of paper that does not bounce. Make up the rules and play the game, if possible.
2. Make a board game (materials needed, construction paper, scissors, tape, ruler, glue, stapler, magic markers, pencils).
3. Plan a campaign to elect Barney, the dinosaur, as the student body president (or similar office). Incorporate any resources that are available to the group in the plan.

Processing the Activity:

1. Who took the initiative to organize the group?
2. Which person contributed the most toward getting the task done? What was the nature of the contribution?
3. Which individuals allowed the others to do the majority of the work?
4. Which individuals, if any, worked to get everyone involved in the project?
5. Would it have been easier to do the task as individuals, or was there some advantage to utilizing the combined resources of the group?

Notes About this Activity:

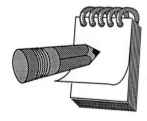

_____

_____

_____

_____

_____

_____

_____

Activity 9

Solving Problems Collectively

Introduction:

When we work together, we have greater resources for solving problems. Cooperative learning requires that we give up the idea of competing with each other and work together to achieve a common goal.

With the creative energies of a group, solutions to problems can be generated. Although there may be competition within the group concerning the best ways to proceed, when we work together problem solving can be more effective and efficient than when we work alone.

Purpose:

- To demonstrate that the sum of a group's efforts is greater than the sum of individual efforts
- To illustrate cooperative learning strategies

Materials:

- One envelope with 5 squares of cardboard and one copy of the Cooperative Problem-Solving Assignment in it for each group or individual, paper and pencil for each to keep score

Time:

- 10 minutes

Educational Media Corporation®, Box 21311, Minneapolis, MN 55421-0311

Procedure:

1. Introduce the activity by telling the participants that problem solving is generally more efficient if it is done as a group rather than as individuals.

2. Select one or more groups of from 5 to 8 individuals to demonstrate cooperative learning strategies. These groups will compete against the remaining individuals to demonstrate the power of a group working together.

3. Assign each group or individual a score keeper. Each competing unit should receive an envelope with five cardboard 3-inch squares in it.

4. Give each competing unit a copy of the instruction sheet and discuss the instructions with them. When ready, tell them to begin.

Processing the Activity:

1. Were there any individuals that scored higher than the groups?

2. What made it easier for the groups to accomplish the task?

3. Which individuals within the groups contributed the most to the group's progress?

4. What, if anything, was done by any individual within the groups to slow or retard progress?

5. What kinds of tasks are best done by groups? By individuals?

Notes About this Activity:

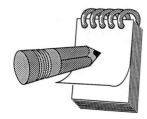

Cooperative Problem-Solving Assignment

1. In your envelope are five 3-inch squares. Your task is to arrange the five squares so that at least one side of each square touches completely one side of another square.

2. There are ten possible combinations. You must use all five squares each time. Mirror or rotated images of a design would give you more than 10 and are *not* acceptable.

3. Your observer should sketch each design before you move on to the next one. Inform the timekeeper when you are finished.

4. Here is a sample. Now, find the other 9.

Educational Media Corporation®, Box 21311, Minneapolis, MN 55421-0311

Answers to Cooperative Problem Solving

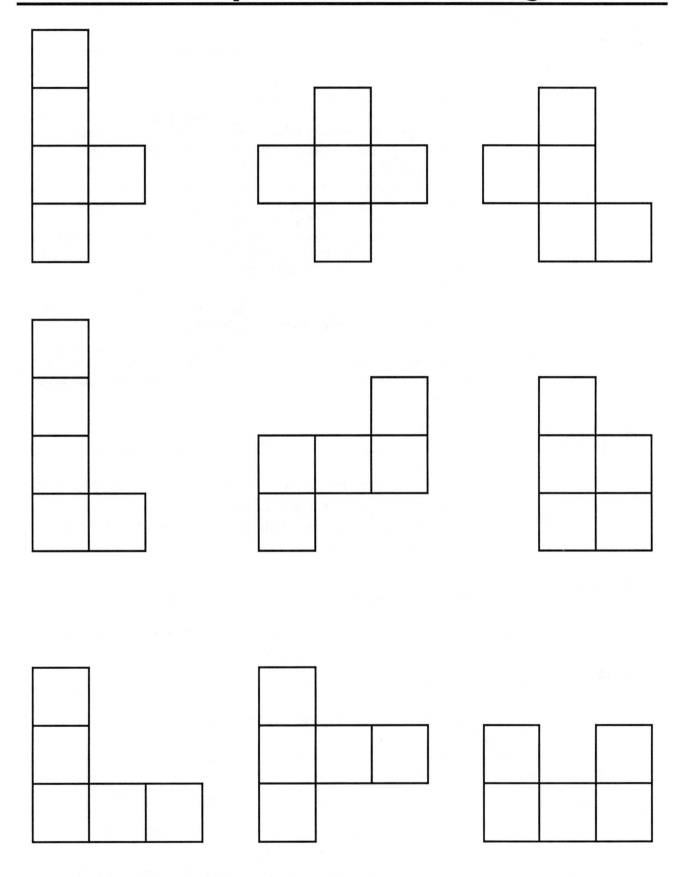

Activity 10
Choosing New Colors

Introduction:

We can learn a lot about ourselves and others by observing the behavior of a group that has a particular task to accomplish. Some members of the group will be preoccupied with the task or assignment. Their energies will be allocated to accomplishing the goal—solving the problem or completing the assignment. Persons interested in the goals of the group are usually called **task oriented.**

Fortunately for the group there also will be some members that are concerned with the wellbeing of the individuals in the group. They are interested in maintaining the interpersonal relationships so necessary for the group to function. These individuals are called **people oriented** because they are interested in maintaining the group's cohesiveness by focusing on the *feelings* of those involved.

Cooperative learning requires that the group have *both* a task orientation and a people orientation to be successful. These orientations are provided by the active participants in the group.

Group members who pay careful attention to the needs of the individuals while at the same time keeping the group focused on the task will no doubt be acknowledged by the group for their contributions as leaders.

Purpose:

- To demonstrate how leaders emerge in problem-solving situations
- To illustrate how solutions can be negotiated
- To provide an awareness of the need for both task and people orientations in a group

Materials:

- Role-play assignment cards for each member of the small group

Time:

- 15 minutes, plus time to process the activity

Educational Media Corporation®, Box 21311, Minneapolis, MN 55421-0311

Procedure:

1. Divide the participants into groups of from 7 to 10. A set of role play cards is required for each small group.

2. Inform the group that they will be experiencing some of the group dynamics present when there is a task to be accomplished. Remind them that it is important that they take the task seriously for the activity to have the maximum impact.

3. Read the problem to the group. Make sure they understand the assignment.

   > Your town has been growing fast. For years there was only one high school, but next year a new school will open, and you are on a committee to discuss creating an identity for the new school. Your group has decided to discuss possible school colors for the new school teams. Each of you will receive a role-play assignment. The success of this exercise depends upon your following the instructions on the card you are given. *Do not reveal what is printed on your card until you are instructed to do so at the end of the exercise.*

4. Distribute the role-play cards to each of the participants. If you have less than ten, eliminate the last cards. Make sure you distribute cards 4 and 7. Remind them *not reveal what is printed on their cards until they are instructed to do so at the end of the exercise.*

5. Allow 10 minutes for the discussion on selecting the colors. If the group finishes too soon, it is probably because one or more participants did not follow the role-play instructions.

6. At this time ask the group to select a leader to take the group through the next phase of the activity. Ask them to discuss the qualifications of each person as demonstrated in the activity and to reach a consensus concerning the leader. Encourage them to select the person best qualified to lead their group.

Processing the Activity:

1. What were the role-play instructions for the person chosen as the leader? Did the activity work as intended? If not, what might have caused the group to choose someone who did not have the specific instructions to behave in a way to be *perceived* as a leader?

2. Which roles were easiest to assume? (Task oriented roles focus on information; people oriented roles focus on what others feel.)

3. What could you do to improve your attention to the needs and feelings of others?

4. What behaviors contributed most to the blocking of the group's efforts to reach its goal?

Role Play Cards

Copy and cut—one set for each group

Copy & Cut

Assignment

Your town has been growing fast. For years there was only one high school, but next year a new school will open, and you are on a committee to discuss creating an identity for the new school. Your group has decided to discuss possible school colors for the new school teams. Each of you will receive a role-play assignment. The success of this exercise depends upon your following the instructions on the card you are given. *Do not reveal what is printed on your card until you are instructed to do so at the end of the exercise.*

1. You favor blue and white. Develop a strong position for these colors. Give as much information as you can to support these school colors.

3. Listen to what colors the others like. Seek the opinions of others. Support any combination of colors that includes red.

2. First, listen to what others think. If someone is not offering a suggestion, ask that person what he or she thinks. Later in the discussion, introduce the idea of different colors like orange and black.

4. You have the special knowledge that it is not important what colors are selected. However, you are to participate in the group in such a way as to be helpful in getting the group to function. Do whatever you can to keep the process running smoothly. At the end of the exercise, the group will be asked to choose a leader. Conduct yourself in a manner that will encourage them to select you for this position.

Educational Media Corporation®, Box 21311, Minneapolis, MN 55421-0311

Copy
& Cut

5. You don't care what the colors are as long as they do not include red.

8. You don't like white. You don't have any particular colors in mind, but you don't want one of them to be white. Develop a strong position against white.

6. You kind of like green and yellow. You can be influenced by a good argument.

9. Blue is your favorite color. Listen carefully to what others say before offering a combination of blue and some other color.

7. You have the special knowledge that it is not important what colors are selected. However, you are to participate in the group in such a way as to be helpful in getting the group to function. Do whatever you can to keep the process running smoothly. At the end of the exercise, the group will be asked to choose a leader. Conduct yourself in a manner that will encourage them to select you for this position.

10. Choose your favorite colors, build a strong case for them, and hold your ground.

Activity 11
Getting Everyone Involved

Introduction:

Problem solving is often approached with confusion. We deal with problems constantly—sometimes well, sometimes badly. If there were no problems, our lives might become stagnant. While we may not always actively seek problems, we can rise to the challenges when they occur.

It is possible to become set in our ways and to lose our effectiveness as problem solvers. By being aware of a variety of problem-solving strategies, we can handle most of the problems we confront with ease. Each new problem requires that we approach it with a fresh awareness—avoiding generalities and stereotypes that might interfere with our effectiveness.

Problem solving can also encourage personal and group change, reduce boredom, stimulate interest, spark curiosity, and provide avenues for bringing solutions into the open. Similar to the team cohesiveness that develops in sports contests, working together to solve a problem can also produce group cohesiveness.

Sometimes there are group members who choose to avoid working within a group. They are defining their relationship within the group as *lose/win.* Running away or avoiding a problem by ignoring the problem, withdrawing, or denying their feelings are seldom useful solutions. When they choose to avoid, they choose to lose. Perhaps they may feel that their relationship within the group is not worth maintaining, but more likely they choose to lose because they *believe* they lack sufficient skills to make a meaningful contribution.

Purpose:

- To demonstrate that cooperation is required to solve problems where one person within the group does not possess all of the information
- To learn to eliminate unnecessary information in problem solving
- To experience the dynamics of cooperative learning and the emergence of leadership

Materials:

- One copy of the Time and Distance Problem sheet for each member, 26 information cards, copied from the following pages and cut to size.

Time:

- 30 minutes

Procedure:

1. Divide the larger group into groups of from six to twelve participants. You will need a set of materials for each small group.

2. Arrange the room so that each small group is sitting in a circle.

3. Introduce the concept that sometimes it takes a group to solve a problem because no one individual has all the information necessary for the solution. The purpose of this activity is to demonstrate the importance of including all of the group members in the process. The participants will learn something about how they—and others—function in a group problem-solving situation.

4. Give each participant a copy of the Time and Distance Problem sheet and read it to them.

> For years our government has been trying to get Americans to switch to the metric system. Highway signs are appearing that show the distance to the next city in kilometers as well as miles. However, many who were raised with inches and miles as ways of measuring distances find the transformation difficult. This activity is designed to demonstrate how difficult some changes can be. Your group task is to find out how long a trip took using different terminologies for time and distance. Pretend that **metas** and **wurts** represent a new way of measuring **distance**, and that **slogas, tars,** and **curns** represent a new way of measuring **time**. You are on a trip with the school band. Your bus travels from town A through towns B, C, and D. How many **tars** did the entire trip take? You have 15 minutes.
>
> *You may read the information on your card(s) to the group, but you may not show or give any of the cards to others. Hint: Not all of the information may be necessary to solve the problem.*

5. Distribute the cards randomly to the participants until all 26 have been distributed. Tell them that their 15 minutes begins *now*. Call time at the end of 15 minutes, even if the solution has not been found.

Processing the Activity:

1. Which persons in the group contributed the most to the solution? What was done that was helpful?

2. Which individuals persisted in their approaches and were detrimental to the group in finding a solution? What approaches were counterproductive?

3. Which individuals appeared to withdraw from working on the problem? What are some of the reasons that might cause someone to quit or withdraw?

4. What information was not needed to solve the problem?

5. What part did a knowledge of mathematics play in your ability to solve the problem? At what grade level were you taught the necessary math skills for this problem?

6. What feelings did you experience during the problem-solving exercise? What behavior evoked the feelings on your part?

7. What role(s) did you play in the group as you worked on the task?

Notes About this Activity:

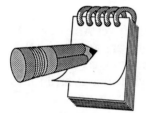

_____

_____

_____

_____

_____

_____

_____

The answer is:	A to B	B to C	C to D		
Distance (metas)	6	12	16		
Time (tars)	18	24	24		
Change to common denominators—	8/24	12/24	16/24	=	36/24= 1 1/2 tars

Educational Media Corporation®, Box 21311, Minneapolis, MN 55421-0311

Time and Distance Problem

For years our government has been trying to get Americans to switch to the metric system. Highway signs are appearing that show the distance to the next city in kilometers as well as miles. However, many who were raised with inches as miles as a way of measuring distances find the transformation difficult. This activity is designed to demonstrate how difficult some transitions can be. Your group task is to find out how long a trip took using different terminologies for time and distance. Pretend that *metas* and *wurts* represent a new way of measuring **distance**, and that *slogas, tars,* and *curns* represent a new way of measuring **time**. You are on a trip with the school band. Your bus travels from town A through towns B, C, and D. How many *tars* did the entire trip take? You have 15 minutes.

You may read the information on your card(s) to the group, but you may not show or give any of the cards to others. Hint: Not all of the information may be necessary to solve the problem.

Copy
& Cut

Time and Distance Problem

For years our government has been trying to get Americans to switch to the metric system. Highway signs are appearing that show the distance to the next city in kilometers as well as miles. However, many who were raised with inches as miles as a way of measuring distances find the transformation difficult. This activity is designed to demonstrate how difficult some transitions can be. Your group task is to find out how long a trip took using different terminologies for time and distance. Pretend that *metas* and *wurts* represent a new way of measuring **distance**, and that *slogas, tars,* and *curns* represent a new way of measuring **time**. You are on a trip with the school band. Your bus travels from town A through towns B, C, and D. How many *tars* did the entire trip take? You have 15 minutes.

You may read the information on your card(s) to the group, but you may not show or give any of the cards to others. Hint: Not all of the information may be necessary to solve the problem.

Copy
& Cut

How far is it from point A to point B?	It is 6 *metas* from point A to point B.

Copy
& Cut

How far is it from point B to point C?

What is a *meta*?

It is 12 *metas* from point B to point C.

A *meta* is 10 *wurts*.

How far is it from point C to point D?

What is a *wurt*?

It is 16 *metas* from point C to point D.

A *wurt* is a way of measuring distance.

Educational Media Corporation®, Box 21311, Minneapolis, MN 55421-0311

How many *wurts* are there in a mile?	What is a *tar*?
There are 4 *wurts* in a mile.	A *tar* is 5 *curns*.
What is a *sloga*?	What is a *curn*?
A *sloga* is 10 *tars*.	A *curn* is a way of measuring time.

How many *curns* are there in an hour?

How fast does the bus travel from town B to town C?

There are 4 *curns* in an hour.

The bus travels from town B to town C at the rate of 24 *metas* per *tar*.

How fast does the bus travel from town A to town B ?

How fast does the train travel from point C to point D?

The bus travels from town A to point B at the rate of 18 *metas* per *tar*.

The train travels from point C to point D at the rate of 24 metas per *tar*.

Educational Media Corporation®, Box 21311, Minneapolis, MN 55421-0311

Activity 12
Dividing Discs, Desserts, and Deserves

Introduction:

Problem solving often requires that we overcome our preconceived notions and inhibitions in order to come up with creative solutions. One key to solving many problems is to pay attention to the details of the *specific* situation and avoid making assumptions that are only implied. These false assumptions limit our options.

We must take a fresh look at each situation to determine the best approach to solving difficult problems. In some situations, breaking a difficult task down into smaller units can be both literally and figuratively necessary.

Brain teasers are activities that keep us alert and require that we look for creative approaches to problem solving. This same creativity also is necessary when we work to resolve our conflicts with others—to generate solutions that are acceptable to both.

Purpose:

- To demonstrate creative problem-solving techniques
- To show that assumptions can be inhibiting
- To learn to divide a problem into smaller parts

Materials:

- A copy of the Discs, Desserts, and Deserves handout for each individual or group, pencils

Time:

- 20 minutes, plus time to process the activity

Procedure:

1. This activity can be done in small groups or by individuals. Provide a copy of the Discs, Desserts, and Deserves handout for each participating unit.

2. Call attention to the circle. Ask how many pieces they can cut it into by making only *four* straight cuts with a long knife.

3. Next, focus their attention on the cake—a three-dimensional object. Ask, "How many pieces can they cut the cake into by making only *four* straight cuts with a long knife?"

4. Point out how preconceived notions, (i.e., the pieces must be equal) limited the creative solutions available.

5. Present the following problem.

   A father has a piece of land. He is getting ready to retire and he loves his four sons. He believes each *deserves* an equal share of his property. To keep peace (or is it pieces?) in the family, each of the plots of land must be the same size *and shape.* All of the land given to each son must be in one piece—the land cannot be distributed in small, broken sections.

6. Call time when the majority of the groups have come up with a solution.

Processing the Activity:

1. How many pieces could you get by cutting the circle with four straight cuts? How many pieces could be cut in a three-dimensional object like a cake?

2. What difficulties did you have in dividing the land?

3. What could have been added to the instructions to make the task easier?

4. Was there an underlying assumption that made the task more difficult? (i.e., that the pieces should be equal.)

5. What experiences from your past made it difficult or easy to solve the problems?

6. How would you classify these types of problems?

7. What rules or principles might you use in solving similar problems?

8. Which person in your group contributed the most to the solutions?

9. Was any individual's behavior a hindrance to reaching a solution?

Educational Media Corporation®, Box 21311, Minneapolis, MN 55421-0311

Discs, Desserts, and Deserves

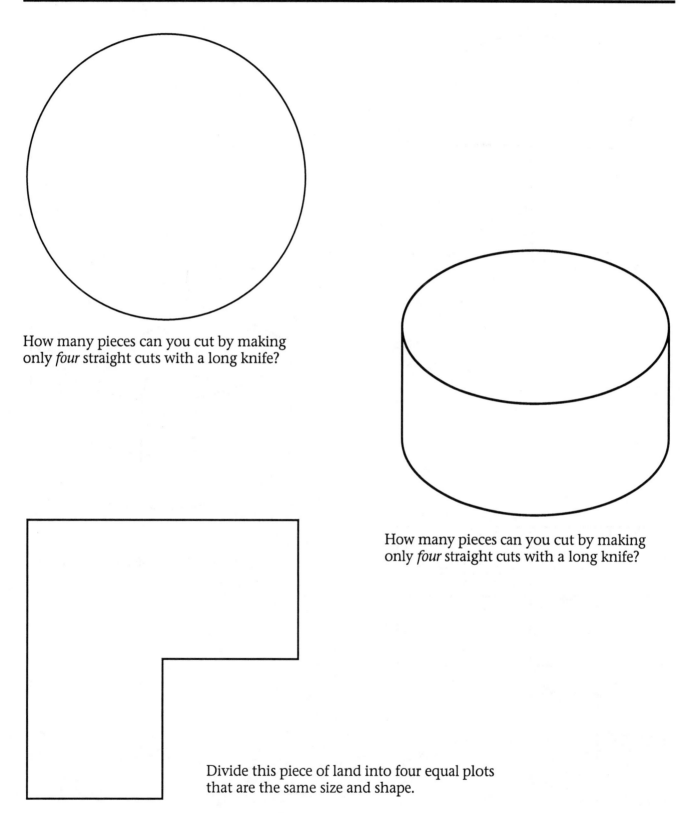

How many pieces can you cut by making
only *four* straight cuts with a long knife?

How many pieces can you cut by making
only *four* straight cuts with a long knife?

Divide this piece of land into four equal plots
that are the same size and shape.

Discs, Desserts, and Deserves Answers

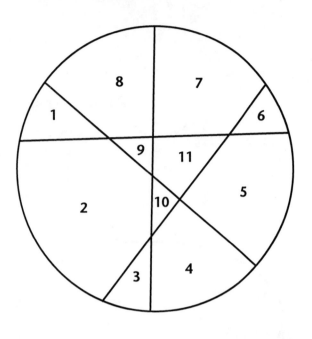

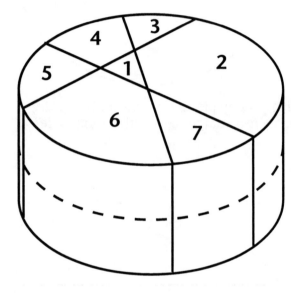

The fourth cut is through the middle creating 14 pieces.

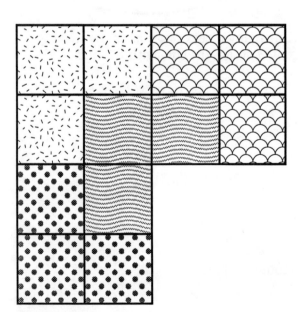

Educational Media Corporation®, Box 21311, Minneapolis, MN 55421-0311

Activity 13
Seeing Isn't Always Believing

Introduction:

Whenever two or more people are gathered together, differences in perception are bound to occur. These differences often lead to conflicts.

We are products of our environments, of our ancestry, and of our experiences. Twin siblings growing up in the same household have different experiences. Their parents have no difficulty recognizing the uniqueness of each personality. Each twin has a different way of perceiving the world, and conflicts between them will inevitably result.

For some of us our perceptions are affected by *genetic differences*. People who are color blind definitely perceive some things differently from those who are not. Differences in perceptions will always exist because of inherent differences in our genetic and experiential backgrounds.

For a conflict to be experienced, it first must be perceived. Have you ever heard the expression, "I can't see the forest for the trees?" By attending to the details, we sometimes miss the big picture.

The purpose of this exercise is to demonstrate that stimuli can be experienced differently by any two people. Our experiences and our perceptions can also either facilitate or inhibit our ability to find solutions to problems.

Purpose:

- To demonstrate differences in our perceptions
- To illustrate the blocks our perceptions can be to problem solving

Materials:

- Copies of the visual stimuli

Time:

- Variable, depending upon the number of examples used

Procedure:

1. Perceptual differences and their impact on problem solving can be experienced in small groups of two or three persons.
2. Provide worksheets for each group and ask them to work together.

Figure/ground Perceptions:

1. When we perceive something as an object, we see it as a definite *figure* against a formless *background*. In the following illustration, what is the figure and what is the background? If you focus on the *white* as the figure, what do you see? If you focus on the *black*, what do you see? You can see two different figures, depending on your focus.

2. Focus on the black arrow below that is pointing down. Carefully turn the page until you see a word. To see the word, you have to change your perception of the figure from being black to being white. Changing your focus in this way is like coming around to another's point of view.

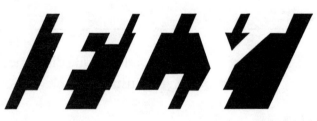

3. Can you get this staircase to invert? Try perceiving one end of a step as being closer to you than the other end. Then reverse your perception and make that end farther away.

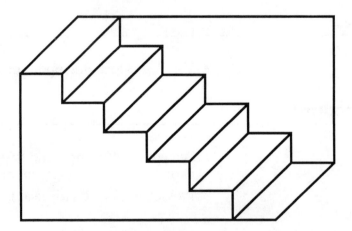

Biased Perceptions:

Your perceptions can be influenced by past learning. The following illustration might be seen as an old woman or a young lady. When shown this illustration for the first time, 60 per cent see the young lady. If people are shown either one of the illustrations on page 56 first, their ability to see the corresponding person in this picture increases dramatically. We see what we are taught to see.

Perceptual Illusions:

Sometimes we organize what we see erroneously. When we perceive our physical environment in a way that does not correspond with reality, we are experiencing a perceptual illusion. Here are some examples of perceptual illusions.

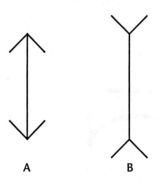

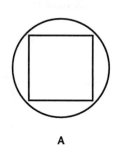

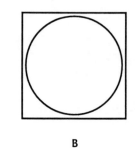

1. Which line is longer, A or B?

2. Which is longer, the horizontal length of the brim or the vertical height of the hat?

3. Which circle is larger, A or B?

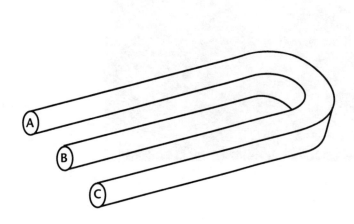

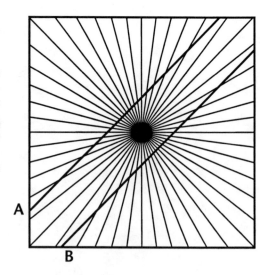

4. How is the B prong connected to A and C?

5. Are lines A and B parallel?

Educational Media Corporation®, Box 21311, Minneapolis, MN 55421-0311

Perceptual Problem-Solving:

Some of the problems we are asked to solve are difficult because our perceptions limit the possible solutions. Solve the following:

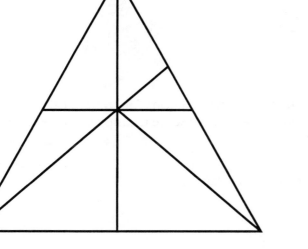

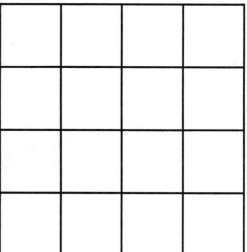

1. How many triangles are there in this diagram?

2. How many squares can you draw within this square?

3. Draw four straight lines through the nine dots without retracing and without lifting your pen from the paper.

Educational Media Corporation®, Box 21311, Minneapolis, MN 55421-0311

Functional Fixedness:

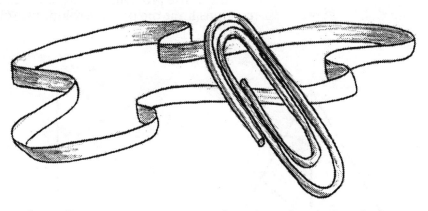

Sometimes we cannot see new functions for an item because we are too focused on a common usage. Give some examples of new ways of using the following:

    a.   book

    b.   inner tube from a car tire

    c.   pliers

    d.   hair pin

    e.   rubber band

Biased Perceptions:

Old Woman

Young Lady

Educational Media Corporation®, Box 21311, Minneapolis, MN 55421-0311

Perceptual Problem-Solving Answers

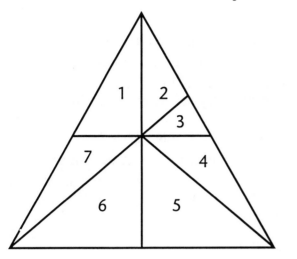

1. 1
2. 2
3. 3
4. 4
5. 5
6. 6
7. 7
8. 1+2+3
9. 2+3+4
10. 3+4
11. 3+4+5+6
12. 5+6
13. 7+1+2
14. 6+7+1
15. 2+3+4+5
16. 2+3
17. 1+7
18. 1+2+3+4+5+6+7

There are a total of 18 triangles.

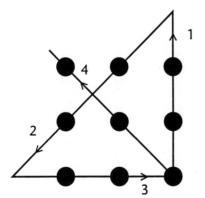

1. 1
2. 2
3. 3
4. 4
5. 5
6. 6
7. 7
8. 8
9. 9
10. 10
11. 11
12. 12
13. 13
14. 14
15. 15
16. 16
17. 1+2+5+6
18. 3+4+7+8
19. 9+10+13+14
20. 11+12+15+16
21. 5+6+9+12
22. 2+3+6+7
23. 10+11+14+15
24. 7+8+11+12
25. 6+7+10+11
26. 1+3+5+6+7+9+10+11
27. 2+3+4+6+7+8+10+11+12
28. 5+6+7+9+10+11+13+14+15
29. 6+7+8+10+11+12+14+15+16
30. 1+2+3+4+5+6+7+8+9+10+
    11+12+13+14+15+16

There are a total of 30 squares.

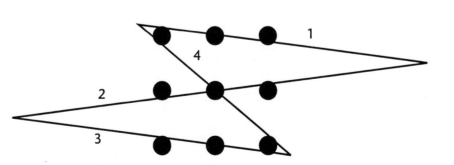

Processing the Activity:

1. Was it difficult for you to reverse your figure/ground perceptions?
2. Could you think of some new uses for common items?
3. Which did you see first, the old woman or the young lady? What did the others in your group do or say so you could finally see the other image?
4. What blocked your attempts at problem solving?
5. What can you do to overcome perceptual differences with another?
6. How can you see something familiar with a fresh approach? Should you also take a new look at others with whom you have become very familiar?

Notes About this Activity:

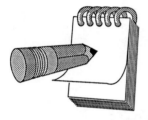

_____

_____

_____

_____

_____

_____

Educational Media Corporation®, Box 21311, Minneapolis, MN 55421-0311

Activity 14
Mapping Our Worlds

Introduction:

What we do, say, and feel is not based on what is happening in the real, *objective* world, but rather, it is based on an internal, *subjective* model of that world which we have created.

Each of us creates a representation of the world in which we live—that is, we create a *map* or *model* inside our head which we use to generate our behavior. Although we live together in a world we all share, our separately created maps or models of that world mean that we all live in somewhat different realities.

These internal models are multi-dimensional. They contain information obtained from all of our senses including *visual* (seeing), *auditory* (hearing), *kinesthetic* (touch and feeling), and *gustatory/olfactory* (tasting and smelling).

Purpose:

- To understand the relationship between maps or models and reality
- To build a map or model of something to share with others

Material:

- Paper, pencil, lemons, blindfolds

Time:

- 30 minutes

Procedure:

1. Introduce the group to the concept that we all have a map or model of the world in our heads. In our memories are sights, sounds, feelings, tastes, and smells stored and available for retrieval when needed. Each of our maps is different, based on our own unique experiences.

2. In building our models, we use symbols to represent the real external world. A road map is an example of a *visual* symbol. To demonstrate the use of visual symbols, ask the participants to draw a map illustrating the route they take from school to their home.

3. Words are *auditory* symbols used to build our models. Pair the participants and ask them to tell their partners how to get from school to home. As the one partner uses words to describe the route, the other partners draw a visual map based on the instructions. The person giving the verbal instructions can watch the map being drawn and suggest appropriate changes. Change roles so both partners can present their models.

4. The *kinesthetic* portion of our model contains our feelings—what we feel through our sense of touch, and what we feel emotionally because we are sensitive—and sometimes touchy. To demonstrate our sensitivity to touch, divide the large group into small groups of 8 to 10 people. Give each participant a lemon and a blindfold. With blindfolds in place, ask them to take a few minutes to get acquainted with their lemon, using only their sense of touch. They should feel the uniqueness of their particular lemon. Call time and ask them to return the lemons to a basket (one basket for each group). With the blindfolds still in place, pass out the lemons at random and ask them to pass them around within the group until they believe they have their original lemon back. To demonstrate the importance of feelings in our internal models, ask the participants to make an entry in their journals about an event that occurred recently. After writing about the event, ask them to underline all of the feeling words used.

5. Our models also contain *smells* and *tastes* experienced in daily living. With blindfolds in place again, pass around a number of bowls covered with cellophane with holes to permit the aromas to escape. Choose a number of items that give off aromas and see if the group members can identify them. Onions, cut fruit, flowers, and chemicals can be used. Do not choose anything that could be harmful if spilled or inhaled.

6. Close by reminding the group that our internal maps or models can and do contain information from visual, auditory, kinesthetic, and olfactory/gustatory sources.

Processing the Activity:

1. Which do you rely on most in building your internal model—visual, auditory, kinesthetic or olfactory/gustatory?

2. Which of the senses would be the most difficult for you to do without?

3. What difficulties, if any, did you have in telling someone how to draw a map to get to your home?

Educational Media Corporation®, Box 21311, Minneapolis, MN 55421-0311

Activity 15
Sharing Our Maps

Introduction:

While our internal models or representations of the world contain cues or symbols based on all of our senses, each of us tends to have a *primary* sensory mode.

If we want to communicate effectively with someone, it is important that we establish a certain rapport. One way of establishing rapport is to determine the sensory mode the person is operating from and meet that person in that modality.

We can obtain clues about the other's operating mode by listening to the words being used. If the person is operating in a *visual* mode, words relating to seeing will be used.

see	picture	show
perspective	glimpse	pretty
colorful	hazy	bright
focus		

In the *auditory* mode, the speaker's words will center around sounds.

listen	hear	talk
shout	loud	harmony
call	yell	tell
noisy		

A person operating in the *kinesthetic* mode will use feeling words.

feel	touch	tense
hurt	pressure	irritated
pushy	relaxed	firm
clumsy		

Even though it may be our intent to speak to a person about feelings, we first should establish rapport by meeting the individual in the current operating mode—and then direct the discussion to the kinesthetic mode by discussing feelings.

Example:

Speaker: I just can't *see* myself as a college student.

Listener: You are having trouble *picturing* what it would be like to go to college. How would it *feel* to earn a college degree?

Purpose:

- To identify primary operating modalities
- To practice meeting people in their current operating system

Materials:

- One copy of the Cues to Sensual Modalities handout for each participant, pencils

Time:

- 30 minutes

Procedure:

1. Introduce the concept of identifying which sensory modality a person is operating in by listening to the words being used.
2. Distribute a copy of the Cues to Sensual Modalities handout to each participant.
3. Brainstorm additional words that could be added to each list.
4. Ask the participants to identify the mode in which the individual is operating in each of the sentences on the handout.
5. Divide the group into triads. Decide who will be the first talker, listener, and observer.
6. Ask the talker to share something that is of current concern. The observer should identify whether the talker is currently operating in the visual, auditory, or kinesthetic mode by the words used. When the talker confirms that the observer is correct, the listener then responds in the same mode, using either visual, auditory, or kinesthetic words in the response.
7. After meeting the talker in the same model, the listener should interject a feeling-focused response. The observer should note whether or not the talker responds to the feeling-focused response with feeling words.
8. Change roles so everyone gets a chance to be a talker.

Processing the Activity:

1. Was it difficult to identify the modality in use?
2. Which modality was the primary one for most talkers?
3. Did you have any difficulty introducing feelings into the discussion?

Educational Media Corporation®, Box 21311, Minneapolis, MN 55421-0311

Cues to Sensual Modalities

Visual	Auditory	Kinesthetic
see	listen	feel
picture	hear	touch
show	talk	tense
perspective	shout	hurt
glimpse	loud	pressure
pretty	harmony	irritated
colorful	call	pushy
hazy	yell	relaxed
bright	tell	firm
focus	noisy	clumsy

The Eyes Have It

Check whether the person is operating in a visual (V), auditory (A), or kinesthetic (K) mode for each statement below.

V   A   K   1. It really hurt when you left me off your team.

V   A   K   2. Let's discuss this like mature people.

V   A   K   3. I hear what you are saying.

V   A   K   4. It is unclear to me what you mean by that.

V   A   K   5. I told you that it didn't matter, but you wouldn't believe me.

V   A   K   6. Keep things in perspective, don't forget what got you here.

V   A   K   7. Reach out and touch someone.

V   A   K   8. You can talk all you want, it won't make any difference.

V   A   K   9. I had a glimpse of what it would be like when we are married.

V   A   K   10. Can't we learn to get along in harmony?

V   A   K   11. I'm under a lot of pressure these days.

V   A   K   12. That was a pretty colorful description of the event.

V   A   K   13. I'm relaxed, don't pressure me.

V   A   K   14. I wish you could see it my way.

V   A   K   15. Didn't you hear anything I said?

V   A   K   16. Let's discuss it.

V   A   K   17. It is clear as mud.

V   A   K   18. Why don't we just forget it. You don't seem to be able to get the picture.

V   A   K   19. Don't be so touchy.

V   A   K   20. I told you this activity wouldn't be any fun.

Activity 16
Eyeing the Eyes

Introduction:

Another way of being able to access and understand the unique models of others is to watch their eye movements. It has been said that the eyes are the mirrors of the mind. It is through the eyes that we sometimes are given clues as to whether a person is functioning in the visual, auditory, or kinesthetic mode. By carefully observing eye movements, we can better understand the processes at work inside of the minds of others.

We can tell if what we are saying is being received by others by observing their eye movements. Even though they might not say anything, their eye movements can provide confirmation that our communication has been received.

Purpose:

- To learn the significance of eye movements coupled with verbal communication
- To know when our communication is being received and processed
- To enhance our abilities to relate to others through non-verbal means

Material:

- One copy of the Eying the Eyes Chart for each participant

Time:

- 20 minutes

Educational Media Corporation®, Box 21311, Minneapolis, MN 55421-0311

Procedure:

1. Review the visual, auditory, and kinesthetic dimensions of our internal models.
2. Distribute a copy of the Eyeing the Eyes Chart and discuss how eye movements reflect the sensory modality being used.
3. When the eyes are raised, the individual is usually operating in the visual mode, either remembering or constructing a visual image internally. When the eyes move from left to right, usually audio cues are being remembered or constructed. When the eyes are lowered to the right (right handed individuals), the individual is in touch with feelings.
4. Pair up the participants. One person is to demonstrate eye movements by responding to the communication of the other. Remind them that the eye movements will come immediately upon hearing the instructions. The person reading an instruction should commit it to memory before speaking in order to maintain eye contact and not miss the eye movements.
5. Switch roles so both partners can observe the eye movements of the other.

Processing the Activity:

1. Did you have any difficulty observing the eye movements of your partner?
2. Can you tell if someone is remembering something (visually) or trying to imagine something?
3. Which of the eye movements was hardest to detect?
4. If you know someone is watching your eyes, can you hide your eye movements?
5. What things did you do to catch your partner off guard?
6. How would this information be useful in communicating on a one-to-one basis?

Notes About this Activity:

_____

_____

_____

_____

_____

_____

Eyeing the Eyes Chart

Eye movements (most right handed individuals)

Up to the right
Visually constructing a model

Up to the left
Visually remembering a model

Horizontal to the right
Auditorily constructing a model

Horizontal to the left
Auditorily remembering a model

Down to the right
Getting in touch with feelings
Kinesthetic model

Down to the left
Getting in touch with tonal differences
in auditory communication

Sample Statements

1. When you were twelve years old, what was your room like?
2. What would you look like in a dress? In a gorilla suit? In a tub full of shaving cream?
3. Tell me about your mother.
4. Could you lead the singing of the National Anthem before a crowd in a stadium?
5. What did you grandfather's voice sound like?
6. What was your first day in high school like?
7. How does this exercise make you feel?

Educational Media Corporation®, Box 21311, Minneapolis, MN 55421-0311

Activity 17
Retrieving Missing Pieces

Introduction:

When we share our models of our world with others, we often take short cuts—leaving out important pieces that are essential to understanding.

Since many people really do not listen to others with the intent of understanding, they let these short cuts stand unchallenged. They are too busy thinking about what to say next rather than really listening.

Good listeners—people who want to know and understand where others are coming from—have learned a few simple techniques to retrieve the pieces that are missing from the model—important information that was glossed over or omitted.

One technique is to *ask for a clarification of pronouns.* It is not always clear whom the speaker is referring to when words such as they, he, she, and them are used. Good listeners never assume they know who is being referred to when pronouns are used. When in doubt, ask the speaker for a clarification.

Generalizations and stereotypes are often used in communication. What these generalizations or stereotypes mean to the speaker may not be what they mean to the listener. Good listeners *ask for specifics whenever the speaker generalizes.* If you ask for an example when the speaker is not specific about something, there is less opportunity for misunderstanding.

Purpose:

- To retrieve missing pieces of a model
- To learn to clarify the use of pronouns
- To explore the specifics upon which generalizations are based

Material:

- One copy of the Incomplete Map, one copy of the More Complete Map, and one copy of the Map Questions sheet for each participant, pencils

Time:

- 30 minutes

Procedure:

1. Discuss with the group the concept that when we share our models or maps with others, often there are important pieces missing that are essential for understanding.
2. Distribute copies of the Incomplete Map. Ask if they can identify the area of the United States this map represents. What additional information would they like to have on the map to make it useful?
3. Distribute copies of the More Complete Map. Note that both maps are symbols which represent the real world. The Incomplete Map should be copied on transparent paper so it can be placed over the More Complete Map.
4. Distribute the Map Questions sheet and ask the participants to answer the questions by placing the Incomplete Map Segments on the More Complete Map. Some of the questions *cannot* be answered from the information on the maps.
5. Discuss the concept of clarifying pronouns and challenging generalizations in order to obtain more information about a person's internal model.
6. Distribute the Retrieving Pieces of the Model worksheet. Discuss the examples and complete the exercise.

Processing the Activity:

1. What additional information would you like to have on the Incomplete Map to make it useful?
2. If you needed to find your way around this state, which map would you rather have?
3. What elements are necessary in a good road map?
4. What questions would you ask to gain more information about the exercise on the Retrieving Pieces of the Model worksheet?

Educational Media Corporation®, Box 21311, Minneapolis, MN 55421-0311

Incomplete Map

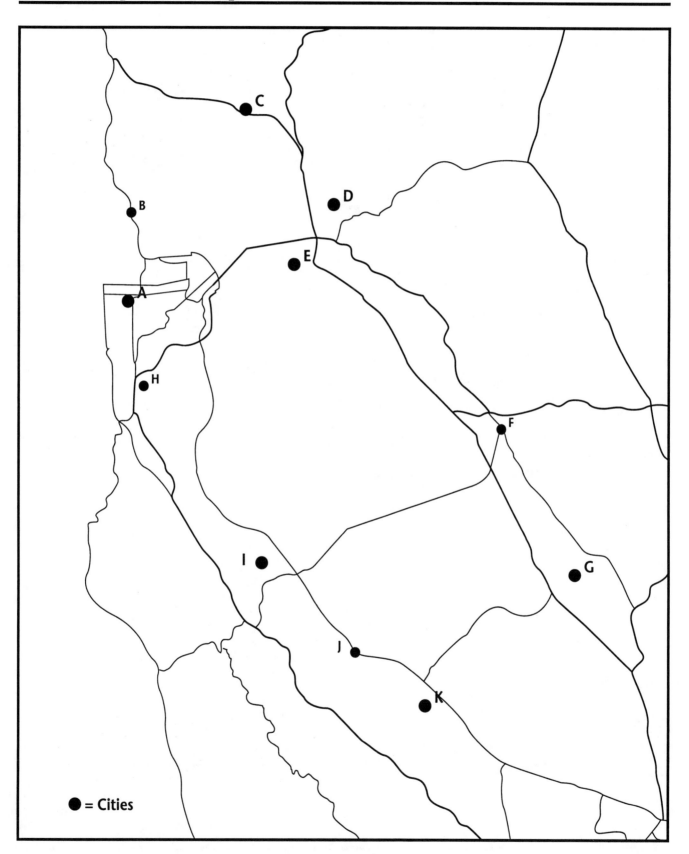

● = Cities

More Complete Map

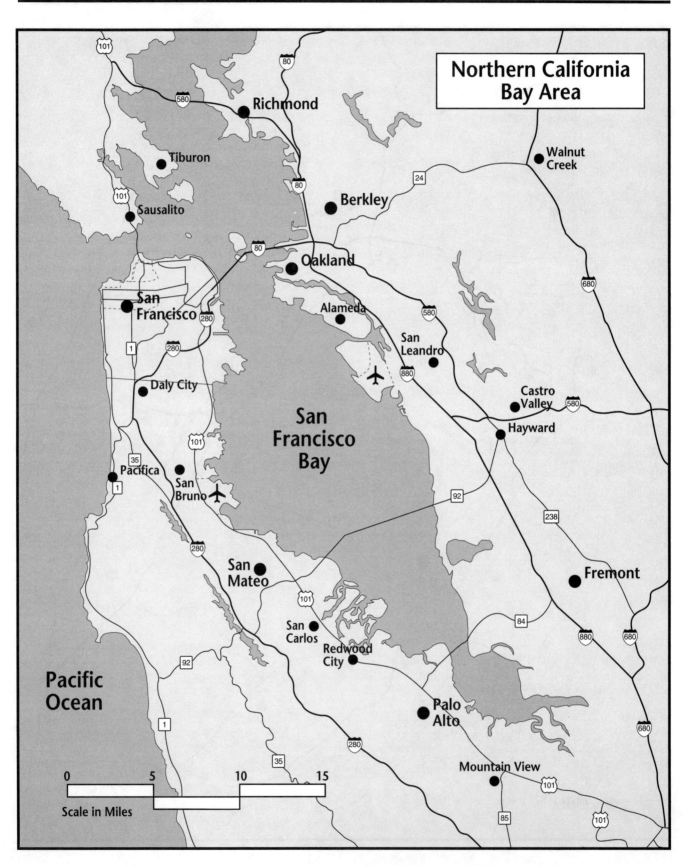

Northern California
Bay Area

101

80

580

Richmond

Tiburon

Walnut
Creek

101

24

Sausalito

Berkley

80

Oakland

80

680

San
Francisco

280

Alameda

580

San
Leandro

1

280

880

Daly City

Castro
Valley

580

San
Francisco
Bay

Hayward

101

92

Pacifica

238

1

San
Bruno

280

San
Mateo

Fremont

101

84

San
Carlos

880

680

Redwood
City

92

Pacific
Ocean

Palo
Alto

1

280

Mountain View

101

35

85

101

| 0 | 5 | 10 | 15 |
Scale in Miles

Educational Media Corporation®, Box 21311, Minneapolis, MN 55421-0311

Map Questions

Using only the information provided on the Incomplete Map and the More Complete Map, answer the following questions:

1. On the Incomplete Map, we refer to a city as City A. What is the name of that city? _____

2. What is the name of City B? _____

3. What is the name of bridge connecting City A with City B? _____

    _____

4. What is the name of City K? _____

5. What famous university is located in City K? _____

6. What is the name of City D? _____

7. What interstate highway would you take if you were driving the shortest route between City D and City G? _____

8. Approximately how far is it between City D and City G? _____

9. What is the name of the city located between City I and City K? ___

    _____

10. Which highway would you take to drive from City I to City K? ____

    _____

11. What is the largest city in *population* on this map? _____

12. What is the largest city in *area* on this map? _____

Did you remember to answer the questions using the information available to you from the maps, not from your own knowledge?

Retrieving Pieces of the Model

Example 1:

Erik and Juan have been friends for years. Erik's parents have lived in the neighborhood all of their lives. Juan lives with his mother and two younger sisters. *They* enjoy playing together after school. Without a father in the home, there isn't the stability there should be.

1. Who enjoys playing together after school?

   A. Erik and Juan

   B. Juan's two younger sisters

   C. Can't be sure from the information given

2. Who does not have a father living in the home?

   A. Juan and his two sisters

   B. Erik

   C. Can't be sure from the information given

3. With whom does Erik live?

   A. Erik's dad

   B. Erik's mom

   C. Erik's dad and mom

   D. Can't be sure from the information given

Example 2:

When I get through with *this*, I'm going to Disneyworld. I can *never* get enough *time* for myself. I am *always* under *pressure*. Hard work should pay off, but it seem like the *only reward* is more work.

Sample questions you might ask to retrieve some missing pieces:

1. What does the word "this" refer to?

2. What would you like to do for yourself that you can't seem to find time to do?

3. What kinds of pressure are you under?

4. What reward would you like?

Exercise:

Write some questions you might ask to retrieve more information about this situation:

It has been a long time since I saw her. She was always special to me. We used to spend a lot of time together, but that was before the accident. I feel responsible, but I don't know what to do about it.

_____

_____

_____

_____

Educational Media Corporation®, Box 21311, Minneapolis, MN 55421-0311

Activity 18
Entertaining Conflicts

Introduction:

Conflicts abound in our lives. When we watch a movie or a television show, we are entertained as the characters work through a conflict. The writers of the show call this the plot. Oftentimes the script contains more than one plot, just as life itself is never simple.

We can learn a great deal about conflict management by reviewing the plots and sub-plots of our favorite shows, examining how the characters handle the various conflicts.

Purpose:

- To identify conflicts that exist in the scripts of motion picture and television shows
- To utilize the entertainment media as a learning experience relating to conflict management

Materials:

- A television and theater guide listing current television shows and movies, a copy of the Entertaining Conflicts Questionnaire for each participant, pencils

Time:

- 30 minutes

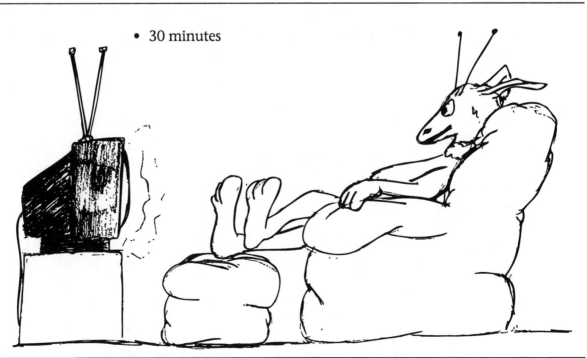

Procedure:

1. Ask the group to brainstorm the names of their favorite motion pictures and television shows. List these on the blackboard. Identify the favorites of the group.

2. Discuss the features that make their favorite shows so successful.

3. Working independently, ask each participant to choose one of the five favorite shows and complete an Entertaining Conflicts Questionnaire concerning that show.

4. After the questionnaires are completed, divide into smaller discussion groups based on the shows selected. If more than six select one show, sub-divide that group to keep the groups small.

Processing the Activity:

Discuss the responses to the questionnaire in small groups.

Notes About this Activity:

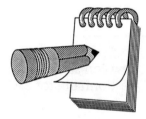

_____

_____

_____

_____

_____

_____

_____

Educational Media Corporation®, Box 21311, Minneapolis, MN 55421-0311

Entertaining Conflicts Questionnaire

Name of the show _____

1. What was the major conflict or plot of this show? _____

   _____

   _____

   _____

   _____

2. What caused the conflict? Shortage? Misunderstandings? _____

   _____

   _____

   _____

   _____

3. How was the conflict resolved? _____

   _____

   _____

   _____

   _____

4. Was the conflict resolved peacefully or violently? _____

   _____

   _____

   _____

   _____

5. How realistic was the solution? Is that the way you believe it would
   have been resolved in real life? _____

   _____

   _____

   _____

   _____

6. Did anything positive result from the conflict?_____

   _____

   _____

   _____

   _____

Activity 19
Journaling Your Conflicts

Introduction:

The best source of examples to help us to understand conflicts is our own personal lives. Authors are often advised to write stories based on their own life experiences. The best plots for television and movie scripts come from real life situations. By beginning a regular program of listing the conflicts we experience in our daily lives, we will accumulate a wealth of information on conflicts and how they are resolved.

Purpose:

- To document the application of problem-solving strategies in real life
- To evaluate personal approaches to problem solving

Materials:

- A notebook—spiral bound or 3-ring for recording observed conflicts

Procedure:

1. Tell the participants that keeping a personal journal of the conflicts in their own lives is one way of helping them to learn more about resolving conflicts. By reflecting on their experiences as they write, their insights into their own approaches to resolving conflicts can be evaluated and improved.

2. For each conflict that they journal, have them respond to the following:

   Who was involved?

   Where did it happen?

   What was the problem?

   What was said/done?

   Did the conflict end constructively/destructively?

3. Ask them to date all entries and remember to make daily entries.

4. Offer the option to also collect articles from newspapers and magazines about conflicts in society and to mount them in a scrapbook.

5. Remind the class that the journals are confidential. If this is part of a class, assign points to determine a grade based on whether or not the assignment is completed, not on the content of the entries.

6. Discuss what additional entries could be included in their journals to make them more useful as a tool to aid in learning cooperative learning and conflict management skills.

Processing the Activity:

1. Discuss what is meant by a *confidential* journal.

2. Decide what should be done by the owners to protect the security of their journals.

Notes About this Activity:

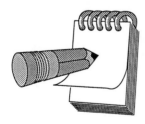

_____

_____

_____

_____

_____

_____

_____

Activity 20

Standing on Your Values

Introduction:

Conflicts arise because we all have different ideas, values, and perceptions. Understanding the positions of others on critical issues is one step in managing conflicts. When we understand and respect the positions of others—and receive respect and understanding for our own stands—we are less threatened by others.

Sometimes we do not know where we stand on certain issues. Unless we have been confronted, we may not have given an issue enough thought to determine our position. To clarify our own positions on certain issues, it is beneficial to listen to the ideas and reasoning of others.

Purpose:

- To demonstrate the variety of positions held by others on particular issues
- To encourage the participants to take a stand for their feelings, beliefs, and values
- To provide an opportunity to hear the thinking and reasoning of others

Materials:

- A room with a minimum of furniture to allow for the physical movement of the participants to the various corners

Time:

- 20 minutes

Educational Media Corporation®, Box 21311, Minneapolis, MN 55421-0311

Procedure:

1. Begin with the participants standing in the center of the room. Share with them one of the items listed on the following page. Designate each corner of the room for individuals with a particular stand on an issue. Corners should be named: strongly agree, agree, disagree, and strongly disagree. Ask the participants to move to the corner that represents their opinion on this issue. Those who are undecided or who have no opinion should remain in the center of the room.

2. Once the group has divided itself on an issue, ask for volunteers to share their reasons for selecting a particular stand. Group members may change corners anytime they wish.

3. Repeat the process by using the issues on the following page or make up your own.

Processing the Activity:

1. Which individuals moved the most rapidly to their chosen corners?
2. Were there some individuals who waited until others moved before taking a position?
3. Did some individuals spend more time in the center of the room than others?
4. How flexible are you concerning controversial issues?
5. Were you swayed by the arguments of others? Who was the most persuasive?

Notes About this Activity:

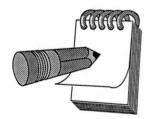

_____

_____

_____

_____

_____

_____

_____

Take a Stand On....

1. It is better to follow your own choice for a career, even if your parents are not in favor of it.

2. We all need some spiritual values in our lives.

3. It is better to work at a job that pays a lot of money than one that you enjoy.

4. You can't work part time and still maintain a position on the honor role (Bs or better).

5. College graduates don't make that much more money in a lifetime than people who start with an employer right after high school.

6. The hassles of having sex before marriage are not worth it.

7. Living in a one-parent family is no different than living with both parents.

8. Only children (no siblings) don't have any special advantages over children with brothers and sisters.

9. It doesn't matter what college you go to. Getting a degree is all that matters.

10. Only students that can't get accepted at a college or university go to technical schools or community colleges.

Educational Media Corporation®, Box 21311, Minneapolis, MN 55421-0311

Activity 21
Brainstorming

Introduction:

Innovative thinking and problem solving are often dampened by the phrases or put-downs of others. Brainstorming is a relatively simple strategy for cultivating creativity and problem solving. The basic ground rules of brainstorming are:

1. No criticizing or judging.
2. Spontaneity and free-wheeling are encouraged (the wilder the idea, the better).
3. Quantity, not quality, is desired.
4. Combining and refining ideas are encouraged.

Purpose:

- To experience creative problem-solving through brainstorming
- To avoid judgmental and critical responses

Materials:

- None

Time:

- 15 minutes

Procedure:

1. Introduce the concept of brainstorming. Remind the group of the rules.
2. Allow 60 seconds for the group to list all of the ways they can for using a common item such as a paper clip or a rubber band. Have someone in the group keep track of the number of responses, not the specific ideas.
3. At the end of one minute, ask the group to report the number of ideas presented, then a sample of the more creative uses suggested.
4. Repeat the process by presenting a problem of concern to the group. Brainstorm possible solutions. Appoint someone to record all suggestions.
5. Choose two or three of the most plausible suggestions for further discussion.

Processing the Activity:

1. How difficult was it to avoid criticizing and judging?
2. What types of problems can brainstorming make the greatest contribution toward solving?
3. What conditions are necessary within the group for brainstorming to work?
4. Are there any times when brainstorming might not be useful?

Notes About this Activity:

Educational Media Corporation®, Box 21311, Minneapolis, MN 55421-0311

Activity 22
Handling Put-Downs

Introduction:

Anger is an emotional reaction—defensive in nature—that occurs when we are frustrated or attacked. When our anger motivates or challenges us, the results are *constructive*. However, when our anger provokes us to respond in aggressive ways toward others, the results are *destructive*.

While we all have a right to express our thoughts and feelings, we need to be respectful of the rights and feelings of others.

Put-downs are forms of responding aggressively to others that do not respect the rights and feelings of others. One way of lessening the number of conflicts that occur between people is to lessen both the number and the affect of put-downs.

Purpose:

- To illustrate the negative impact of put-downs
- To practice fending off the emotional impact of put-downs

Materials:

- One copy of the Put-Downs handout for each participant, pencils

Time:

- 30 minutes

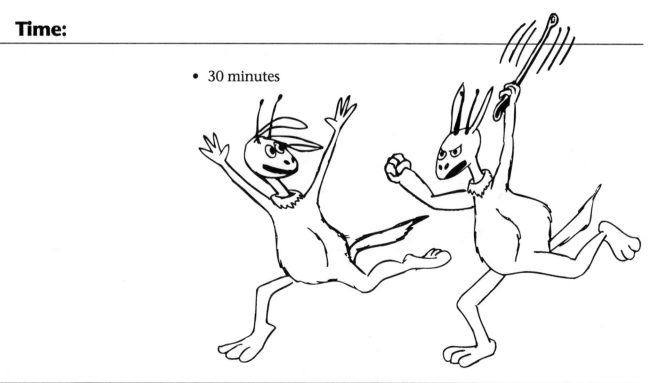

Procedure:

1. Share some thoughts with the group about anger and one way that it is expressed—through put-downs.
2. Hand out a copy of the Put-Downs handout.
3. Discuss ways of handling put-downs.
4. Brainstorm a list of put-downs. Write them on the blackboard so they can been used in this exercise.
4. Divide the group into triads. One person is to read selected statements from the blackboard and the second person is to provide a response that is *not* a put-down. The third person should serve as an observer and score the number of positive responses that are made.
5. Change roles so that each person has a chance to practice responding without giving put-downs.

Processing the Activity:

1. How do you feel when someone puts you down?
2. Which of the five methods of handling put-downs do you use the most?
3. There is a saying, "Sticks and stones can break your bones but words can never hurt you." Do you believe that?
4. Do you believe that you can choose your reactions (feelings) to the behaviors and words of others?
5. How important is it for you to understand how the behaviors of others impact on your feelings?

Notes About this Activity:

_____

_____

_____

_____

_____

_____

_____

Educational Media Corporation®, Box 21311, Minneapolis, MN 55421-0311

Put-Downs

Effective methods of handling put-downs:

1. Ignore the put-down and the person saying it. Do not acknowledge or reinforce what was said.

2. Respond with anything except a put-down. Do not escalate the conflict. Use a comeback that is not aggressive or one that indicates that the put-down did not affect you.

   "I don't accept that."

   "Really? I didn't know that."

3. Agree with the put-down verbally while failing to own the content of the message.

   "You're right. Who told you?"

4. Make a joke out of the put-down.

   "Would you put that in writing for my lawyer?"

5. Instead of thinking about what is being said, focus on what might be going on within the other person:

   A. What is the *real* problem?

   B. What might be happening to give that person negative feelings about self? (Generally, the person making the put-down is *displacing* negative feelings about self.)

   C. What does the person really need?

6. Remind yourself that you do not need to take ownership of what is being said and internalize it.

   A. You know what is really true.

   B. You are an O.K. person regardless of what is said.

   C. You can choose your reactions to the words of others.

Activity 23
Busting Balloons

Introduction:

Many young people believe that violence is the only way they have of dealing with conflicts. In choosing violence, they define their conflicts as *win/lose* propositions. Aggressive individuals who use verbal and physical violence become closed to other alternatives. They lose the ability to recognize that their behavior inflames the conflict rather than resolves it. Their aggressive strategies soon lead to the destructive control of others.

It would be difficult to say there could never be a time in a person's life when aggressive action or violence would be useful. Some believe that violent and aggressive behaviors can act as safety valves to lower tension. Research indicates that the reverse may be true—violence *nurtures* violence. Violent acts result in even greater violence. Violence and aggression tend to increase confusion in a conflict situation. They make each side more rigid, increasing alienation and making meaningful communication impossible.

Purpose:

- To demonstrate the use of aggressive behavior in a team contest
- To allow for the reduction of tension through the use of physical aggression
- To provide a win/lose experience for the group

Materials:

- Different colored balloons for each small group and string to tie the balloons to their ankles

Time:

- 10 minutes, plus time to process the activity

Procedure:

1. Introduce this activity as an opportunity to experience competition as teams. Each team is to determine a strategy to succeed in popping the balloons of the other teams.
2. Form teams of four members each. Each member in the team blows up and ties to an ankle a balloon of the same color.
3. When you give the signal, all players try to break the balloons of the opposing team members. When a balloon is broken, that player must go to the edge of the group and watch the outcome. Any team with a member without a broken balloon at the end is a winner.

Processing the Activity:

1. Did your group work together to break balloons or did each member act independently?
2. What did you learn about yourself in this exercise?
3. What did you learn about your team mates?
4. Now that the activity is over, what might your team have done to have been more effective in winning?

Notes About this Activity:

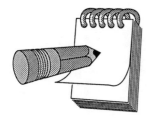

_____

_____

_____

_____

_____

_____

_____

Activity 24
Fighting Presumptions

Introduction:

Since we live in a society where competition is stressed, we generally view tasks as competitive in nature. When we are faced with a task that we presume requires a competitive approach, the number of strategies for responding to the problem are immediately reduced. The notion that there might be another way to approach a situation does not often enter our minds. When we see past competition as a problem-solving method and realize that cooperation also is a valid approach, new energies are released.

Often when we are faced with a new problem or task, we must remember that it is possible that a cooperative approach might be more productive than a competitive one.

Purpose:

- To demonstrate an alternative to a win/lose approach to conflicts
- To illustrate how presumptions influence our ability to see alternative solutions

Time:

- 15 minutes

Materials:

- Table or desk for each pair of participants

Educational Media Corporation®, Box 21311, Minneapolis, MN 55421-0311

Procedure:

1. With very little fanfare or introduction, have the participants choose partners and take seats across from each other over a small table or desk.

2. Ask them to clasp each other's opposite hand, keeping their elbows resting on the table. NOTE: This is the position for arm wrestling, but do not mention arm wrestling or any other competitive game of that nature.

3. Tell the participants that the goal of this exercise is to touch the back of their partner's hand to the table as many times as they can in 30 seconds. Both members of the team should count for themselves.

4. After 30 seconds, call stop and ask for the scores.

5. Share with the group the information in the introduction to this activity.

6. Repeat the instructions, "The goal of this exercise is to touch the back of your partner's hand to the table as many times as you can in 30 seconds."

7. Repeat the 30-second trial and see if the scores improve.

Processing the Activity:

1. Did any of the participants change their approach?

2. How did you feel during each of the sessions?

3. What kept you from choosing a cooperative approach on the first round?

4. Are there times when a cooperative approach would not be the most productive?

Notes About this Activity:

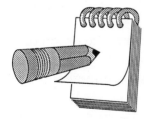

_____

_____

_____

_____

_____

_____

_____

_____

Activity 25
Experiencing Conflicts

Introduction:

Conflicts exist whenever incompatible things happen *between* people. When there are *differences* in information, beliefs, opinions, assumptions, ideas, needs, values, and goals, conflicts exist.

Conflicts also result when there are *shortages* of certain resources such as time, space, money, power, influence, and position.

Competitions or rivalries also produce conflicts. When you are in competition, your goals are in opposition to the goals of the others. You want to win, which means you want your competitor to lose.

Cooperation can also foster conflicts. You can disagree about the best way to achieve the goals you both share.

Conflicts are inevitable, even in the friendliest of groups. A conflict is a moment of truth, a test of a relationship. Conflicts can weaken or strengthen relationships. They are critical events that can bring creative insight and closer relationships—or lasting resentment. Conflicts can push us away from each other or pull us into closer and more cooperative relationships. They may result in aggression or mutual understanding.

We should be careful not to avoid conflicts or to resolve them too soon. We need to explore our differences to better understand ourselves and others. From conflicts emerge the best—or the worst—in us.

Purpose:

- To demonstrate the use of collaborate efforts to win in competitive situations
- To illustrate the effects of success and failure on the selection of group leaders
- To develop an awareness that limits are often self-imposed

Materials:

- Twelve forfeited "bank certificates" (copy and cut page 94), one "closed-bid" envelope for each group of five, one hundred dollars in play money (copy and cut page 93) for each group in denominations of 5, 10, and 20, Tally Sheet, pencil and scratch paper

Time:

- 50 minutes

Procedure:

1. Set the background for this activity by explaining that a local bank is auctioning off a number of savings accounts or "bank certificates" for accounts that have been abandoned. All efforts by the bank to locate the owners or their survivors have failed. These abandoned accounts are being auctioned off to the highest bidder. To have a chance at winning, you are pooling your assets as groups of five. Your assets are in the envelopes which will be distributed shortly.

2. Divide the participants in groups of five each and number each group. Place the different groups in various parts of the room so they can discuss their strategies without being overheard by others.

3. Ask each group to choose one member to act as the spokesperson for the first round of the activity. A different person will be elected (or re-elected) as the spokesperson for each of the rounds to follow.

4. Each group is to arrive at a strategy for winning a bank certificate at the "auction." The spokesperson speaks for the group at the auction. No instructions may be signaled to the spokesperson from the group once the round has begun. Even numbered rounds will be by open bidding; odd-numbered rounds will be by closed bids.

5. Distribute the envelopes that you prepared earlier containing the play money—one to each group. This money will be used to purchase the bank certificates that are put up for auction. No bank certificate will contain less than 25 dollars.

6. Groups are not precluded from collaborating with each other; however, do not draw their attention to this possibility. Let the participants act on their own if this option should become obvious.

7. Announce that the first round will be by *closed* bids. Give them two to three minutes to develop their strategy, then have the spokespersons for each group bring up an envelope with the amount of money they bid in it.

8. Open the bids and award the first bank certificate to the highest bidder. Keep track of the bids and the winnings on the Tally Sheet.

9. Announce that the second round will be by open bidding. Have the groups elect a new spokesperson. Allow two minutes for the groups to discuss their bidding strategy.

10. Have the spokespersons come forward. Oral bids are taken on the second bank certificate. Award the bank certificate to the highest bidder and post the bids and the winnings on the Tally Sheet.

11. Continue the rounds until all 12 bank certificates have been awarded.

Processing the Activity:

1. What did you learn about the strategies necessary to win at the auction?

2. Who in your group contributed the most to your group's bidding strategies?

3. What competition existed within your group even though you shared a common goal?

4. What happened in your group as your resources were depleted?

5. What rules did you assume existed for the game that in actuality did not?

Notes About this Activity:

_____

_____

_____

_____

_____

_____

_____

Educational Media Corporation®, Box 21311, Minneapolis, MN 55421-0311

Spending Money

Copy ✂ & Cut

Bank Certificates

Copy
✂
& Cut

Certificate of Deposit $25	Certificate of Deposit $25
Conflict Managers Savings Bank	Conflict Managers Savings Bank
Certificate of Deposit $25	Certificate of Deposit $25
Conflict Managers Savings Bank	Conflict Managers Savings Bank
Certificate of Deposit $25	Certificate of Deposit $30
Conflict Managers Savings Bank	Conflict Managers Savings Bank
Certificate of Deposit $35	Certificate of Deposit $30
Conflict Managers Savings Bank	Conflict Managers Savings Bank
Certificate of Deposit $40	Certificate of Deposit $40
Conflict Managers Savings Bank	Conflict Managers Savings Bank
Certificate of Deposit $50	Certificate of Deposit $50
Conflict Managers Savings Bank	Conflict Managers Savings Bank

Educational Media Corporation®, Box 21311, Minneapolis, MN 55421-0311

Tally Sheet

Amount Bid / Amount Won

	Group 1	Group 2	Group 3	Group 4	Group 5
Round 1	Won / Bid	Won / Bid	Won / Bid	Won / Bid	Won / Bid
Round 2	Won / Bid	Won / Bid	Won / Bid	Won / Bid	Won / Bid
Round 3	Won / Bid	Won / Bid	Won / Bid	Won / Bid	Won / Bid
Round 4	Won / Bid	Won / Bid	Won / Bid	Won / Bid	Won / Bid
Round 5	Won / Bid	Won / Bid	Won / Bid	Won / Bid	Won / Bid
Round 6	Won / Bid	Won / Bid	Won / Bid	Won / Bid	Won / Bid
Round 7	Won / Bid	Won / Bid	Won / Bid	Won / Bid	Won / Bid
Round 8	Won / Bid	Won / Bid	Won / Bid	Won / Bid	Won / Bid
Round 9	Won / Bid	Won / Bid	Won / Bid	Won / Bid	Won / Bid
Round 10	Won / Bid	Won / Bid	Won / Bid	Won / Bid	Won / Bid
Round 11	Won / Bid	Won / Bid	Won / Bid	Won / Bid	Won / Bid
Round 12	Won / Bid	Won / Bid	Won / Bid	Won / Bid	Won / Bid

Activity 26
Sharing the Wealth

Introduction:

Sometimes conflicts result when there are **shortages** of certain resources such as time, space, money, power, influence, and position.

We live in a competitive society and often resources are limited. There may be only one paper route available in the neighborhood, only one starting quarterback on the team, and only one head cheerleader. In some families there is not enough money for all of the children to afford college, have their own cars, or even to buy new clothes.

This activity is designed to bring to awareness some of the feelings and experiences that result in conflicts due to a lack of resources.

Purpose:

- To demonstrate the effects of a shortage
- To experience a win/lose situation
- To provide an opportunity to experience rejection or exclusion

Materials:

- The participants should be told ahead of time to bring some small change to class. The activity is more effective when the money used is owned by the participants.

Time:

- Allow 10 minutes, plus time to process the activity

Educational Media Corporation®, Box 21311, Minneapolis, MN 55421-0311

Procedure:

1. Divide the larger group into groups of threes.

2. Each person in the smaller group contributes an equal amount of money to a pool in the center of the table. It can be twenty-five cents, fifty cents, or one dollar each.

3. Each group of three is to decide how to divide the money in the center of the table—excluding one person—from the final payoff. Only a maximum of two people in the group will get the money. You cannot use chance methods—drawing lots—nor can you make promises to take care of the third person later. The majority rules. You must divide the money between not more than two people.

4. It should be the objective of each participant to get as much money as possible to experience this activity fully. Each participant should try to convince the others in the group to be given all the money. If two gang up to divide the money, the other should offer one of the others a better deal. Keep the process going for ten minutes. Always give the third person a chance to influence the decision before accepting the final division.

Processing the Activity:

1. How did you handle the situation? Did you give up or work enthusiastically to win?

2. What strategies did you use to influence the others?

3. What did you learn about yourself in this activity?

4. What did you learn about the others?

5. What were your feelings at various stages of this activity?

6. Following the discussion, you might agree to return the funds to their original owners as a way of providing closure to this activity.

Notes About this Activity:

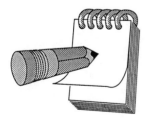

_____

_____

_____

_____

_____

_____

_____

Activity 27
Splitting the Take

Introduction:

Because there is not an unlimited supply of resources, we often must share with others. How we share resources is governed by our perceptions of what is fair and equitable.

When our perceptions of fairness differ, conflicts result. Perceiving that a resource is being shared fairly often is more important than having the resource itself.

When we believe we are being treated unfairly, many times we are willing to do without something rather than accept an inferior portion.

When we negotiate with others, even in a position of power, it is best to create an image of fairness. Although we might be tempted to take advantage of someone on a single exchange, it may be wiser to build a positive relationship with others which will pay off in long-term relationships.

Purpose:

- To demonstrate our perceptions of fairness and equality
- To illustrate some basic principles of negotiating

Materials:

- Something that can be divided: 50 jelly beans, M & Ms or something of similar value and desirability

Time:

- 15 minutes

Procedure:

1. Choose two people to demonstrate this concept before the group. Give the first volunteer (Person A) a container with the items to be divided in it. Person A is to make an offer to split whatever is in the container with Person B.

2. Person A is to make the offer. Person B may only accept or reject the offer. Person B cannot give any input into the offer or negotiate the split. If Person B accepts the offer, the items may be divided.

3. If Person B rejects the offer, neither person gets any of the items.

4. We are often tempted to offer splits that are favorable to us, such as a 60/40 or 80/20 split. While it might be rational for Person B to accept any offer, regardless of how little received, many persons will reject offers that don't seem fair.

Processing the Activity:

1. Did Person A offer an even or equitable split, or was the offer favorable to Person A?

2. How did person B react to the offer? Accept? Reject?

3. Was the benefit of developing a long-term relationship taken into consideration when making the offer?

4. What feelings were evident in both parties involved in the transaction?

Notes About this Activity:

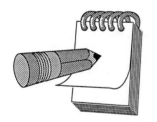

_____

_____

_____

_____

_____

_____

_____

Activity 28
Drafting New Players

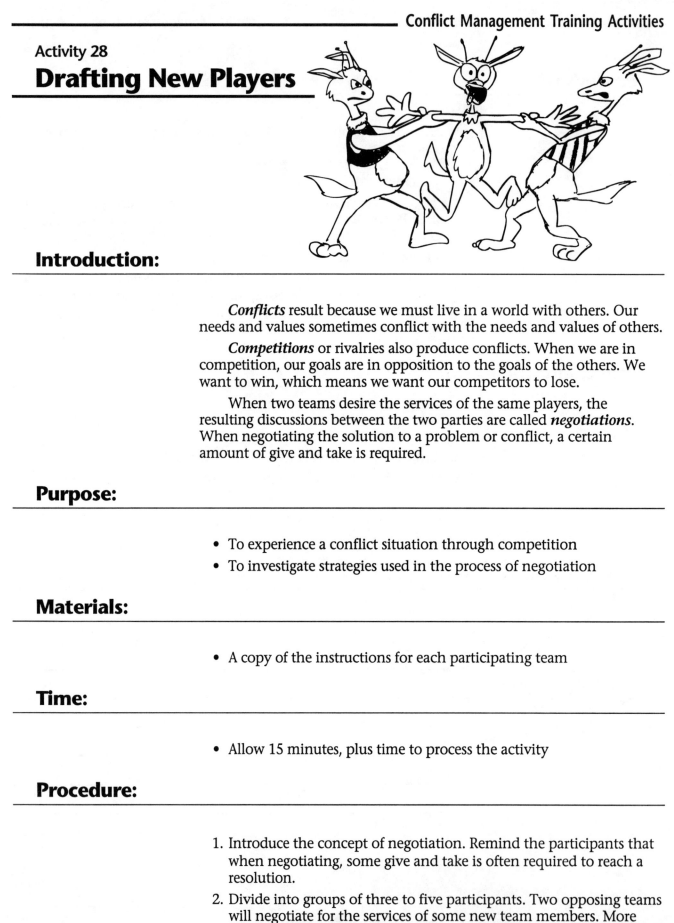

Introduction:

Conflicts result because we must live in a world with others. Our needs and values sometimes conflict with the needs and values of others.

Competitions or rivalries also produce conflicts. When we are in competition, our goals are in opposition to the goals of the others. We want to win, which means we want our competitors to lose.

When two teams desire the services of the same players, the resulting discussions between the two parties are called negotiations. When negotiating the solution to a problem or conflict, a certain amount of give and take is required.

Purpose:

- To experience a conflict situation through competition
- To investigate strategies used in the process of negotiation

Materials:

- A copy of the instructions for each participating team

Time:

- Allow 15 minutes, plus time to process the activity

Procedure:

1. Introduce the concept of negotiation. Remind the participants that when negotiating, some give and take is often required to reach a resolution.
2. Divide into groups of three to five participants. Two opposing teams will negotiate for the services of some new team members. More than one negotiating session can be supervised in the same room at the same time.

Educational Media Corporation®, Box 21311, Minneapolis, MN 55421-0311

3. Each team is to discuss the strategy to be used in the negotiating session and elect a chief negotiator to carry out the strategy. Others on the team can participate, but to reduce confusion, the chief negotiator should do most of the talking.

4. Provide each team with a copy of the instructions and the specific information only that team possesses. Read the instructions to the groups before they begin.

> Your job is to negotiate on behalf of your team with a rival team for five new players. Each of you have the special knowledge of how well each player will perform on your team in the coming year. You may not share this knowledge with your rival negotiator. Once the deals have been arranged, check to see which team was the winner by the number of points the players negotiated for are worth to that team.

	Player	Team A	Team B
1.	_____	_____	_____
2.	_____	_____	_____
3.	_____	_____	_____
4.	_____	_____	_____
5.	_____	_____	_____
6.	_____	_____	_____
7.	_____	_____	_____
8.	_____	_____	_____
9.	_____	_____	_____
10.	_____	_____	_____
TOTAL	_____	_____	_____

Processing the Activity:

1. What strategies did each team use in negotiating for the players?

2. What was necessary to come to an agreement?

3. How did you select the person to be chief negotiator? What special skills should a negotiator have?

4. If you were to repeat the activity, what would your group do differently?

Confidential Instructions for Team A

Your job is to negotiate on behalf of your team with a rival team for five new players. Each of you have the special knowledge of how well each player will perform on your team in the coming year. You may *not* share this knowledge with your rival negotiator. Once the deals have been arranged, check to see which team was the winner by the number of points the players negotiated for are worth to that team.

Team A

Player	Points
1	90
2	80
3	70
4	60
5	50
6	40
7	30
8	20
9	10
10	0

Copy & Cut

Confidential Instructions for Team B

Your job is to negotiate on behalf of your team with a rival team for five new players. Each of you have the special knowledge of how well each player will perform on your team in the coming year. You may *not* share this knowledge with your rival negotiator. Once the deals have been arranged, check to see which team was the winner by the number of points the players negotiated for are worth to that team.

Team B

Player	Points
1	0
2	10
3	20
4	30
5	40
6	50
7	60
8	70
9	80
10	90

Educational Media Corporation®, Box 21311, Minneapolis, MN 55421-0311

Activity 29
Exploring Negotiating Styles

Introduction:

How we perceive or define a conflict or problem affects how we attempt to resolve it.

Win/lose.

If we perceive a problem as a *win/lose* situation, nothing good may result. It may be difficult to ever establish cooperative relationships with others because of the way we perceive the situation. We may build ourselves up, but others will feel resentful and try to cut off communication. Defining a conflict in a *win/lose* manner promotes distrust, dislike, deception, rivalry, and threats. Our relationship will continue to deteriorate as long as we perceive it in this fashion.

Lose/win.

If we perceive the situation as a *lose/win* relationship, we are saying that we do not care enough about the relationship or that we lack the skills to resolve a conflict.

Win/win.

If we perceive our problem as a *win/win* situation, we realize that we both have something invested in the problem and its solution. We see the conflict as something that can be solved by working together for a mutually satisfying solution. Defining the conflict as a *mutual* problem to be solved will increase communication, trust, and respect for each other. No one loses when we sit down to solve a mutual problem.

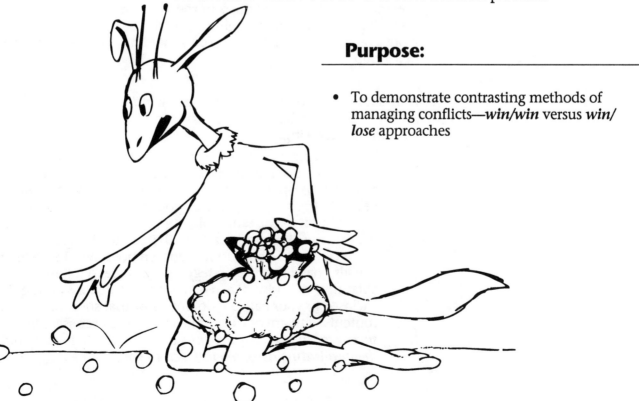

Purpose:

- To demonstrate contrasting methods of managing conflicts—*win/win* versus *win/ lose* approaches

Materials:

- One paper sandwich bag for each participant; 10 assorted colored beads for each participant. Prepare the bags as follows for a group of 12 students. You may have to adjust the proportion of colors for smaller groups.

Bag No.	Red	Blue	White	Green
1	4	2	2	2
2	2	4	2	2
3	2	2	4	2
4	2	2	2	4
5	3	3	2	2
6	3	2	3	2
7	3	3	2	2
8	3	2	1	4
9	2	1	4	3
10	4	3	2	1
11	1	4	3	2
12	2	2	3	3

Time:

- 30 minutes

Procedure:

1. You may use up to 12 members in the same group. If you have more than 12 participants in the training, divide the larger group into groups of up to 12 participants. You should have at least 8 members in a group.

2. Introduce the concepts of *win/win* and *win/lose* problem solving. After you have divided the participants into groups of 8 to 12, explain the following:

   You are being issued a bag containing ten beads of four different colors: red, green, blue, and white. Each bag contains a different proportion of the colors, but each bag contains ten beads. In the next 15 minutes, your objective is to collect fifteen beads of the same color and turn them in at the end of the exercise. If you collect more than 15 for 150 points, you will receive a 15-point bonus for each bead over 15. Each of you also has a specific strategy that you are to follow in obtaining your objective. Follow the instructions on the sheet enclosed in your bag, but do not show that sheet or share its contents with anyone until the end of the exercise. *The success of the exercise depends on your ability to carry out the negotiating assignment given to you.*

3. Place the following instructions in half of the bags:

> Your are to adopt a **win/lose** negotiation strategy in which you are to try to obtain more beads of the same color than anyone else. Some are going to win and others are going to lose. You want to be a winner. The use of deceit, threats, and force may be helpful in negotiating with your group members. Try to achieve the best outcome for yourself, and use your power and skill in any way that helps you do so. Remember, if you keep the other group members from winning, you will increase your chances of winning.

4. Place the following instructions in the other half of the bags:

> You are to adopt a **win/win** negotiation strategy in which you try to define the task and find creative solutions that are satisfying to as many members as possible. In negotiating, try to make the problem solving as creative as possible. Communicate openly and honestly about your needs and try to find ways in which to help both you and other members of the group to experience success. Avoid all threats and deception that might destroy trust among group members. The problem is to figure out how as many group members as possible can complete the task.

5. For an added dimension, place the following instructions in one of the bags:

> You are to adopt a **lose/win** negotiation strategy. When you perceive a situation in this way, you are saying that you do not care enough about the relationship or that you lack the skills to resolve the conflict. Demonstrate that you are not interested in playing the game. You did not wish to collect beads nor are you willing to trade or share your beads with others.

6. Monitor the activity carefully to insure that the different instructions are acted upon but not shared openly with others. At the end of the 15-minute negotiating period, total the scores for those who have collected 15 or more beads of the same color.

Processing the Activity:

1. Ask the participants to share their feelings about the negotiating session.

2. Ask what was learned about each participant as a result of this activity.

3. Divide the group according to the instructions they had for negotiating.

4. How successful were members of the *win/win* group in reaching the objective of 15 or more beads of the same color?

5. How successful were members of the *win/lose* group in reaching the objective of 15 or more beads of the same color?

6. If you had a *lose/win* person, what were the group's reactions?

7. What were the positives and negatives of each negotiating style?

Notes About this Activity:

_____

_____

_____

_____

_____

_____

Educational Media Corporation®, Box 21311, Minneapolis, MN 55421-0311

Win/lose

You are being issued a bag containing ten beads of four different colors: red, green, blue, and white. Each bag contains a different proportion of the colors, but each bag contains ten beads. In the next 15 minutes, your objective is to collect fifteen beads of the same color and turn them in at the end of the exercise. If you collect more than 15 for 150 points, you will receive a 15-point bonus for each bead over 15. Each of you also has a specific strategy that you are to follow in obtaining your objective.

Your are to adopt a *win/lose* negotiation strategy in which you are to try to obtain more beads of the same color than anyone else. Some are going to win and others are going to lose. You want to be a winner. The use of deceit, threats, and force may be helpful in negotiating with your group members. Try to achieve the best outcome for yourself, and use your power and skill in any way that helps you do so. Remember, if you keep the other group members from winning, you will increase your chances of winning.

Do not show this sheet or share its contents with anyone until the end of the exercise. The success of the exercise depends on your ability to carry out the negotiating assignment given to you.

Copy
✂
& Cut

- -

Win/win

You are being issued a bag containing ten beads of four different colors: red, green, blue, and white. Each bag contains a different proportion of the colors, but each bag contains ten beads. In the next 15 minutes, your objective is to collect fifteen beads of the same color and turn them in at the end of the exercise. If you collect more than 15 for 150 points, you will receive a 15-point bonus for each bead over 15. Each of you also has a specific strategy that you are to follow in obtaining your objective.

You are to adopt a *win/win* negotiation strategy in which you try to define the task and find creative solutions that are satisfying to as many members as possible. In negotiating, try to make the problem solving as creative as possible. Communicate openly and honestly about your needs and try to find ways in which to help both you and other members of the group to experience success. Avoid all threats and deception that might destroy trust among group members. The problem is to figure out how as many group members as possible can complete the task.

Do not show this sheet or share its contents with anyone until the end of the exercise. The success of the exercise depends on your ability to carry out the negotiating assignment given to you.

Copy
✂
& Cut

- -

Lose/win

You are being issued a bag containing ten beads of four different colors: red, green, blue, and white. Each bag contains a different proportion of the colors, but each bag contains ten beads. In the next 15 minutes, your objective is to collect fifteen beads of the same color and turn them in at the end of the exercise. If you collect more than 15 for 150 points, you will receive a 15-point bonus for each bead over 15. Each of you also has a specific strategy that you are to follow in obtaining your objective.

You are to adopt a *lose/win* negotiation strategy. When you perceive a situation in this way, you are saying that you do not care enough about the relationship or that you lack the skills to resolve the conflict. Demonstrate that you are not interested in playing the game. You did not wish to collect beads nor are you willing to trade or share your beads with others.

Do not show this sheet or share its contents with anyone until the end of the exercise. The success of the exercise depends on your ability to carry out the negotiating assignment given to you.

Activity 30
Empowering the Beasts

Introduction:

Human interactions involve power or influence. People who are interacting are constantly influencing or being influenced by others. The dynamics of power or influence cannot be ignored in relationships. We should be aware of our power, accept it, and take responsibility for its use. Groups that work together cooperatively to reach a goal are powerful—the members mutually influence each other to do their best.

Power is the ability to get others to behave in the way we desire.

Resistance is a psychological force in an individual that blocks the acceptance of the influence of others.

Manipulation is the use of power to manage or control others in a shrewd, unfair, or dishonest way. Using power for personal benefit at the expense of others is not acceptable in a cooperative learning environment.

Most competitive activities, such as the one that follows, will provide illustrations of *power*, *resistance*, and *manipulation*.

Purpose:

- To experience the frustration of possessing a lack of influence or power in a group
- To demonstrate the tendency to manipulate others for personal gain
- To illustrate how resistance is formed as a reaction to power grabbing

Materials:

- Sacks of colored beads for each player, a set of instructions, blackboard or poster board to keep the results, and name tags with different designations

Time:

- 50 minutes

Procedure:

1. Tell the group that this activity is designed to show the dynamics of interactions among groups of unequal resources.

2. Divide the larger group into groups of eight to ten participants. Each of the smaller groups can be managed in the same room, although they are not to interact with each other.

3. Within each of the smaller groups there will be three sub-groups: the *beasts,* the *bees,* and the *bugs.* The *beasts* have the power by the nature of their size. The *bees* have mobility and can inflict some pain on the beasts, but the lowly *bugs* have little resources and are easily squashed.

4. Through the successful use of negotiation skills, the object of the game is to become (or stay) in the *power* group—the beasts.

5. Each participant is given a copy of the instructions and a bag of six colored beads. Randomly distribute the bags which you have prepared ahead of time according to the following instructions:

   > For a group of 10, you will need 1 yellow, 2 black, and 50 assorted red, white, and blue beads. Divide as follows:

   > 4 bags with 1 yellow, 1 black, and 4 randomly divided red, white, and blue beads

   > 2 bags with 1 black, and 5 randomly divided red, white, and blue beads

   > 4 bags with 6 randomly divided red, white, and blue beads

6. Give the group time to inspect their bags and to understand the instructions. Explain that they will have a negotiating session of two minutes in which to improve their scores.

7. Complete the first negotiating session. Total the scores and award the name badges to the winners. The top three scores get *beast* badges, the middle three become *bees,* and the bottom group are *bugs.*

8. Conduct round two. Take the scores and change the badges. Verbally reward the beasts for their fine work and intensify the frustration of the bees and bugs with your comments.

9. Begin the third negotiating session. You should notice some frustration on the part of the bees and bugs. Nothing they seem to do permits them much upward mobility.

10. Before beginning the fourth session, tell the beasts that they have the power to make the rules for the next negotiating round. Others can make suggestions, but the beasts will make the rules. For example, they can redistribute the wealth so everyone is equal or they can change the rules so the bees and bugs must trade with them.

11. After the new rules have been posted, begin the fourth negotiating session. By now the frustration on the part of the powerless should lead to some resistance, or open rebellion.

12. Before the fifth session, ask the beasts to caucus to see what rules they would like to change. Hand out copies of the Influence Sheet to the bees and bugs.

13. Begin the fifth session. Depending on the level of frustration generated in the low-power groups, during this round you can expect to see anything—cheating, apathy, or open rebellion.

14. Before you lose total control, stop the activity and process.

Processing the Activity:

1. What was it like to be in the low-power groups?

2. What was it like to be a beast?

3. What changes did you notice in individuals as they obtained or retained power?

4. What were some of the strategies used to attempt to advance? Did they work?

5. What strategies did the low-power participants consider in the final rounds?

6. What feelings resulted from the unequal distribution of power?

7. Would it have made any difference if some of the participants who were bugs or bees had drawn bags that would have automatically made them beasts?

8. For many your fate was sealed with the random distribution of the resources in the bags. In what ways is this like real life? In what ways is it not?

Notes About this Activity:

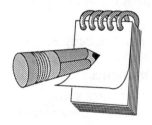

Educational Media Corporation®, Box 21311, Minneapolis, MN 55421-0311

Instructions—Empowering the Beasts

You are a member of a society in which there are three levels of power: the *beasts*, the *bees*, and the *bugs*. Your power is determined by the point value of the beads in your bag. You may advance from one level to the other by obtaining a higher point value through negotiation. The three members with the highest scores at the end of each round will be declared beasts. Each color has a certain point value; additional points are given for having several of the same color:

Color	Points	Number of a Kind	Points
Yellow	50	6	50
Black	25	5	40
Blue	15	4	30
White	10	3	20
Red	5		

Rules:

1. During a 3-minute negotiating session, you can improve your scores by trading.
2. You may only trade one-for-one. A trade consists of trading one bead each of unequal value. Other trading combinations are not permitted.
3. Select a player with whom to trade. Hold hands during the negotiations. If you cannot make any agreement, you must stay connected throughout the round.
4. No talking except to the person whose hand you are holding.
5. If you do not wish to negotiate, fold your arms. You do not have to negotiate during a particular round.
6. All beads must be hidden. Do not show the beads in your bag to anyone.

Influence Sheet

Ways of influencing groups in power:

1. Change the power group's attitudes through education or moral arguments.
2. Use the existing rules to bring pressure for change.
3. Search for ways to make the power group dependent upon the rest of the group.
4. Use harassment techniques to increase the power group's costs of staying with the current procedures.
5. Organize and pool your resources to be less vulnerable.
6. Cheat.

Copy
✄
& Cut

- -

Influence Sheet

Ways of influencing groups in power:

1. Change the power group's attitudes through education or moral arguments.
2. Use the existing rules to bring pressure for change.
3. Search for ways to make the power group dependent upon the rest of the group.
4. Use harassment techniques to increase the power group's costs of staying with the current procedures.
5. Organize and pool your resources to be less vulnerable.
6. Cheat.

Educational Media Corporation®, Box 21311, Minneapolis, MN 55421-0311

Name Tags

Copy
✂
& Cut

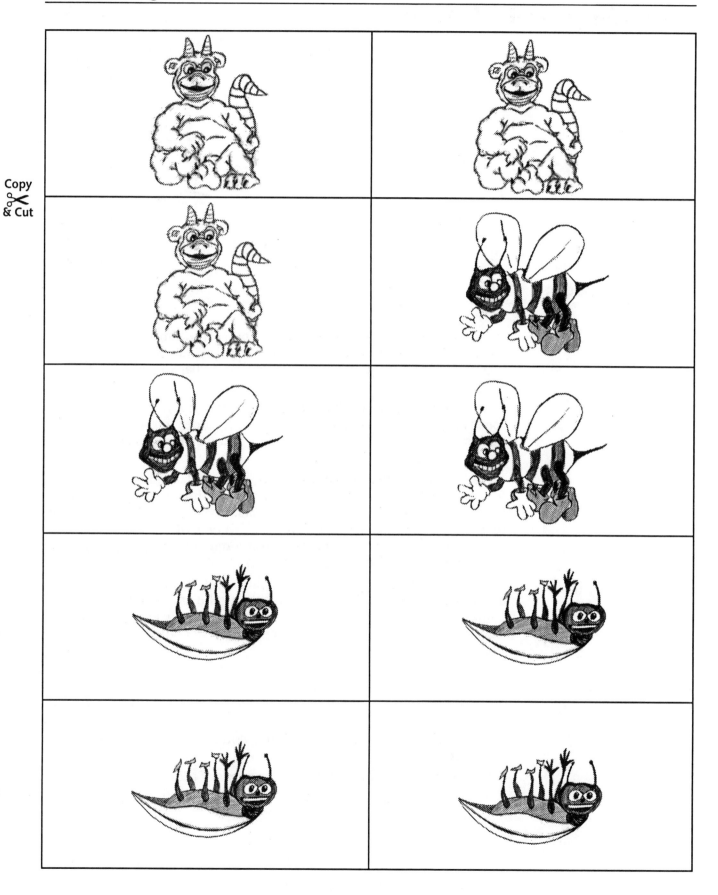

Activity 31
Building Six-Inch Squares

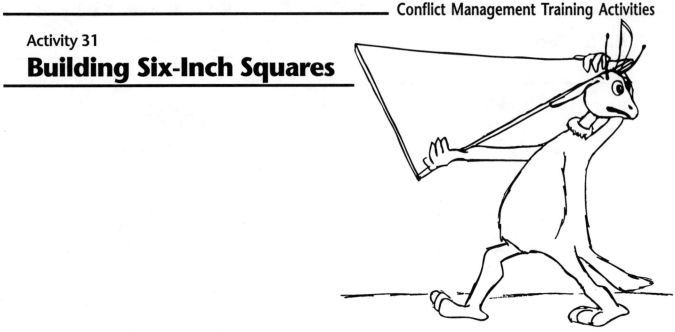

Introduction:

If we want to understand what others are thinking or feeling, we need to tune in to the cues they are sending. In addition to the words they use, communication also occurs in non-verbal and extra-verbal ways.

Extra-verbal communication comes through tone of voice, the speed of speech, pauses, and hesitations. It includes stammering, stuttering, and stumbling, as well as exaggerated emphasis on words or facial expressions.

Non-verbal communication can be conveyed by a turn of the lip, a frown, a rolling of the eyes, or a tapping of the fingers. Body language has been a subject of study for many years. However, there is no reliable reference book that analyzes or explains this type of language. Although we should use caution when making interpretations, it is important to be aware of non-verbal and extra-verbal communication.

As we develop our verbal communication skills, we often pay less attention to non-verbal clues. In this activity the use of verbal communication is banned. Group members must rely entirely on non-verbal communication to reach the group goal of completing five six-inch squares.

Purpose:

- To focus on non-verbal communication as a way of expressing needs
- To sensitize group members to the needs of others
- To recognize that a task is not completed until all of the goals are met

Educational Media Corporation®, Box 21311, Minneapolis, MN 55421-0311

Materials:

- Five six-inch squares cut according to the models provided and placed in five envelopes. The numbers on each piece dictate into which envelope the pieces are put to begin the exercise; tables that will seat 5 people each around them; one set of instructions for each group of five

Time:

- Allow 15 minutes to solve the puzzle, plus time to process the activity

Procedure:

1. Divide the participants into groups of five. You will need a set of puzzle pieces in five envelopes for each small group. If you desire, you can add one or two people to each group to serve as observers. They are instructed not to participate in solving the puzzle, but simply to observe the behavior of the five participants.

2. Introduce this activity by talking about the need for cooperation in a group. List on a blackboard suggestions the group has for being cooperative in working on a group task. Some suggestions that might be discussed:

   a. Understanding the total problem.
   b. Understanding how they can contribute toward the solution.
   c. Understanding the potential contributions of others.
   d. Understanding the problems and needs of others.

3. Tell the group that you have an activity that will test the cooperative concepts they have just listed.

4. Clear off the tables on which the puzzles will be assembled. Pass out the five envelopes and a copy of the instruction sheet to each group. Instruct them not to open the envelopes until you tell them.

5. Read the instructions to all the groups.

   Each of you has received an envelope which contains pieces of cardboard to be used in forming a six-inch square. When I give you the signal, open your envelopes, take out the pieces, and begin the process of putting together a six-inch square. There are enough pieces in all five envelopes to make *five* squares. Each person in the group is to assemble one square. The group task is over when *each* person has a completed six-inch square on the table. Put together your own square. The following *restrictions* are placed on your group for this exercise:

a. No *verbal* communication—no talking or note passing.

b. No person may *ask* another member for a specific piece or in any way *signal* that another person is to give a specific piece. No grabbing or stealing pieces from others.

c. Persons may *give* pieces to other group members to assist them in completing their puzzles, even if they have already completed their puzzles. Do not throw your pieces in the center for others to take.

Reminder: This is a non-verbal activity demonstrating cooperative problem-solving skills.

Processing the Activity:

1. Who was willing to give away pieces of the puzzle?
2. Did anyone finish a puzzle and then withdraw or quit, letting the others complete their puzzles?
3. Was there anyone who continually struggled with the pieces, but was unwilling to give any or all of them away?
4. What non-verbal communication was used?
5. What was the turning point in which the group cooperated and all of the puzzles were completed?
6. Did anyone try to violate the rules to expedite the task?
7. How did the members of the group express their frustrations?

Notes About this Activity:

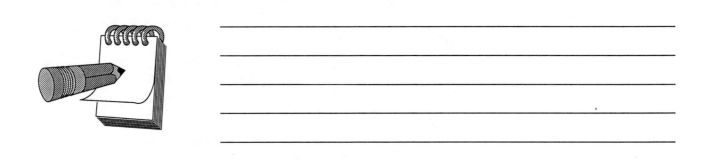

Educational Media Corporation®, Box 21311, Minneapolis, MN 55421-0311

Model for the Squares

Cut five pieces of cardboard into six-inch squares. Using the following models, cut each square and number the parts. Put all of the parts with a number 1 on it in envelope 1, 2 in 2, and so forth. Cut five six-inch squares for each group of 5.

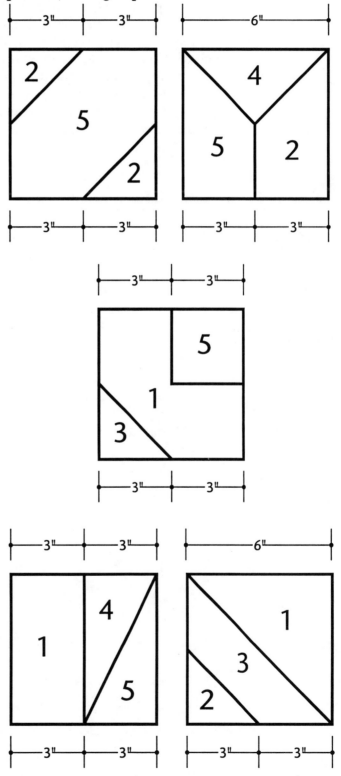

Activity 32
Taking Note

Introduction:

Good listening is not a *passive* act. On the contrary, good listening is an *active* process where we work at understanding what a person is saying. Attending to what another is saying requires concentration. In addition to the verbal responses we make as listeners, our non-verbal behavior also communicates whether or not we are listening.

Good listeners look at the person who is talking, pay attention to the words, and convey their interest and concern with their posture and actions. Good listeners are also aware of the feelings of the person who is talking. When we do respond, we say something that demonstrates that we understand.

Purpose:

- To identify non-verbal communication that interferes with listening
- To practice good listening skills

Materials:

- None

Time:

- 10 minutes

Educational Media Corporation®, Box 21311, Minneapolis, MN 55421-0311

Procedure:

1. Introduce the activity by telling the group that they are going to practice listening skills while getting better acquainted. Remind them to pay attention to what is being said and to keep their responses to a minimum.
2. Divide the group into pairs. One person serves as the talker and one as the listener.
3. Ask the talkers to turn to the listeners and share something about themselves for two minutes. The subject matter is not important, although they should be encouraged to share something personal.
4. At the end of the two minutes, ask the talkers to provide observations about their listeners' non-verbal behavior.
5. Repeat the exercise, changing roles.

Processing the Activity:

1. As a listener, how conscious were you of your non-verbal behavior?
2. What non-verbal behaviors proved to be distracting to the listeners?
3. What non-verbal behaviors seemed to aid the communication?
4. After you knew your non-verbal behavior would be observed, how was your listening affected?

Notes About this Activity:

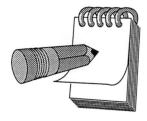

_____

_____

_____

_____

_____

_____

_____

Activity 33
Listening for Dollars

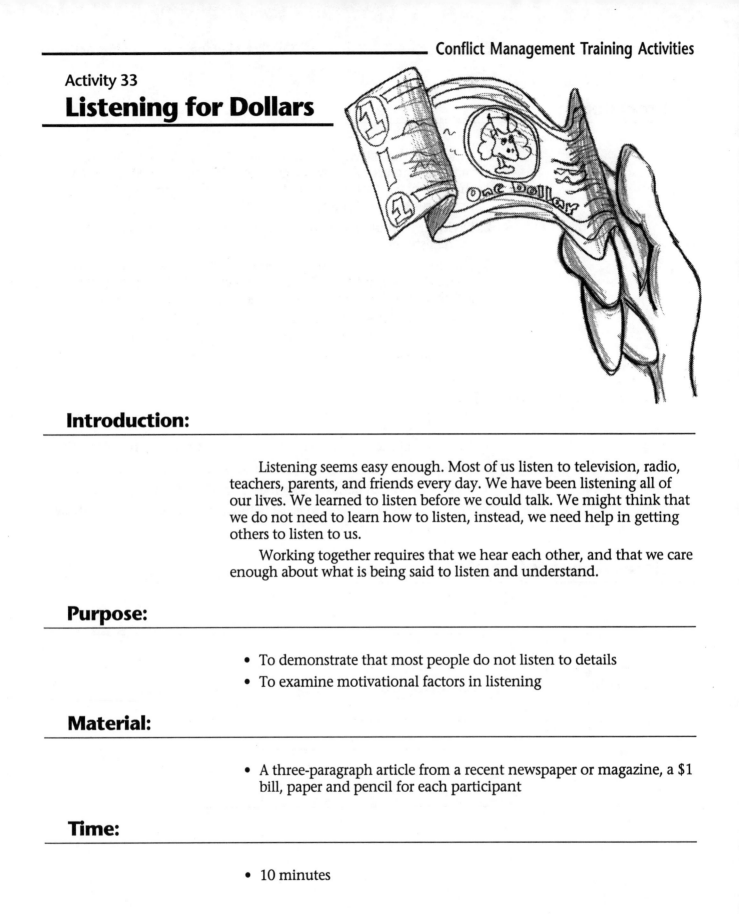

Introduction:

Listening seems easy enough. Most of us listen to television, radio, teachers, parents, and friends every day. We have been listening all of our lives. We learned to listen before we could talk. We might think that we do not need to learn how to listen, instead, we need help in getting others to listen to us.

Working together requires that we hear each other, and that we care enough about what is being said to listen and understand.

Purpose:

- To demonstrate that most people do not listen to details
- To examine motivational factors in listening

Material:

- A three-paragraph article from a recent newspaper or magazine, a $1 bill, paper and pencil for each participant

Time:

- 10 minutes

Educational Media Corporation®, Box 21311, Minneapolis, MN 55421-0311

Procedure:

1. Clip a story from a newspaper or magazine that is approximately three paragraphs long.

2. Do not introduce this activity, simply say "Some of you probably saw this item in the paper the other day." Then read the three-paragraph article out loud. When you are finished, note the reaction of the people in the group.

3. Then, take out a dollar bill and say, "Okay, I've got a few questions for you based on the story you just heard. Whoever gets them all correct wins this dollar."

4. Read seven or eight questions that you prepared ahead of time about the article (details like names, date, place, etc.) In all likelihood, not one person will answer *all* of the questions correctly and you will be able to keep your dollar.

Processing the Activity:

1. Although you all heard the story, few of you could remember many details. Why?

2. What kept you from listening? What can you do to sharpen your listening skills?

3. If you had known in advance that I would be offering a dollar for the information, would you have listened more carefully? Why?

4. What are some things that motivate us to listen to others?

Notes About this Activity:

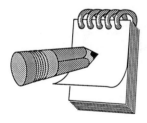

_____

_____

_____

_____

_____

_____

_____

Activity 34
Attending to the Message

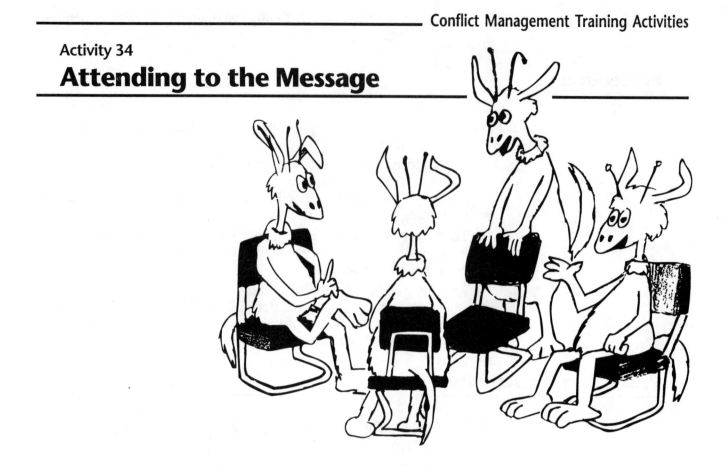

Introduction:

Listening is one of the most important skills we can possess. Yet, oftentimes it appears that there are very few skilled listeners in today's world. It seems that people aren't really interested in what we have to say. Sometimes they are so caught up in their own thoughts they are not able to focus on what we are saying.

While later in the training we will discuss the importance of being able to listen for the *feelings* behind the words, in this activity we are concerned with being able to focus on the *content* of the message.

Purpose:

- To demonstrate miscommunication in the sending of a message from one person to another
- To illustrate difficulties that can result from miscommunication

Materials:

- Tape recorder

Educational Media Corporation®, Box 21311, Minneapolis, MN 55421-0311

Time:

- Allow a minimum of 15 minutes, plus time to process the activity

Procedure:

1. Discuss the importance of listening to the content of what a person is saying and some of the problems that can result when content is misunderstood.
2. Select six people from the group to demonstrate the difficulty in communicating a brief message through six people.
3. Ask all but one of the volunteers to leave the room. Turn on the tape recorder to preserve a record of the transmissions.
4. Read the following message to the volunteer who remained in the room.

   It was awful. I was almost caught right in the middle of an accident. I need to get to the hospital right away.

   An old Chevy was heading south on Central when the pickup, heading north, turned left, right in front of the Chevy. The Chevy sped up, trying to avoid the pickup. I'm not sure which car hit the UPS truck which was just sitting at the stop sign heading east.

5. Ask the second volunteer to return to the room. The first volunteer conveys the message to the second.
6. The third volunteer is asked to return and the message is passed verbally from the second volunteer. Continue until all six volunteers have returned.
7. The sixth person should write the message on the blackboard so it can be compared with the original message.

Processing the Activity:

1. What contributed to the distortion of the message through the six transmissions?
2. What could be done by the listeners to make sure the message is received accurately?
3. What harm could have come from the distortions of this message?

Notes About this Activity:

_____

_____

_____

_____

Activity 35
Misunderstanding Others and Being Misunderstood

Introduction:

Understanding others is an important ingredient in working together in harmony. It creates a certain degree of predictability which is invaluable for maintaining positive relationships. When we understand one another, the chances of conflicts are reduced.

Misunderstanding is a major contributor to relationship problems. The loneliest people in the world are usually people who are frequently misunderstood. Feelings of disappointment, anger, and loneliness are associated with chronic misunderstanding. Misunderstandings often result when we fail to disclose information about ourselves, or when we fail to encourage disclosure in others.

When others do not know about our feelings and thoughts, we increase the chances of being misunderstood. When we do not encourage others to disclose, misunderstandings also are likely to result.

Understanding requires that information be *mutually* disclosed. With only partial disclosure comes partial understanding. Others must guess what is going on inside us, and we must guess what is going on inside others.

Purpose:

- To practice mutually disclosing feelings and thoughts

Materials:

- None

Educational Media Corporation®, Box 21311, Minneapolis, MN 55421-0311

Procedure:

1. Remind the participants of the importance understanding plays in communication.

2. Divide the participants into groups of three. Each of the members will eventually perform all of the roles. One person is to assume the role of observer while the other two agree to be talkers.

3. Choose a value rich area from the accompanying chart. Pick a topic in one of the value rich areas on which the talkers have different points of view.

4. The beginning talker is given one minute in which to express views on a controversial topic. During this time the observer and the other participant listen.

5. Once the first talker stops, the second talker must summarize the key statements made by the previous speaker before offering a point of view. The observer is to insure that an accurate summary of the first talker takes place before the second person expresses a point of view.

6. The two talkers continue to exchange points of view (after summarizing the previous statements of the other) until they agree that each understands the viewpoint of the other.

7. The observer changes places with one of the talkers and a new topic is chosen. Repeat the process until all three members of the group have been observers.

Processing the Activity:

1. How difficult was it to get the second person to summarize the key statements of the speaker before expressing an opinion?

2. What misunderstandings occurred?

3. Did the observer have to intervene at any time?

4. Was any value rich area chosen more than once?

5. Did understanding the other person's view point bring the two parties into closer agreement on the issue?

Notes About this Activity:

_____

_____

_____

_____

_____

Value Rich Areas

Educational Media Corporation®, Box 21311, Minneapolis, MN 55421-0311

Activity 36
Developing a Feeling Word Vocabulary

Introduction:

Our society has a history of repressing feelings. There is a general myth that to be "objective" and "rational" is to rule out all feelings and emotions. Being objective and rational really means that we utilize all available information in making a decision. Feelings are an important source of information.

Everyone has feelings. When we express ourselves, our ideas are always complimented by feelings, either *pleasant, unpleasant,* or *both.*

When others listen to us—and we listen to others—often only the spoken words are heard and the feelings that are communicated are missed. Feelings are a natural part of our lives and should not be ignored. Some feelings may be easily identified because they were referred to when the story was being told. Other feelings are found behind the words. They may be a driving force or an emotional expression that completes the thoughts and ideas.

It is important to listen to a person with whom you have a conflict. Knowing and understanding how the other person feels is important to determining that person's needs and desires.

A practical way to be aware of the feelings of others is to ask, "Am I hearing *pleasant* or *unpleasant* feelings? Or am I hearing *both* kinds of feelings?" This little technique helps us to focus our attention on what the other person is experiencing. It also gives us a hint as to how we might respond.

Purpose:

- To build a vocabulary of words to describe pleasant and unpleasant feelings

Materials:

- A copy of the Feeling Word Vocabulary for each participant, paper and pencil

Time:

- Allow 20 minutes

Procedure:

Begin the activity by having the participants work independently. Give them the following instructions and allow time to complete each phase.

1. Think about a pleasant experience that you have had recently. Now, write down as many feeling words as you can that describe that experience.

2. Think back to a recent unpleasant experience. Write down the feeling words that come to mind as you think about that event.

3. Now, write down as many feeling words as you can that describe how you are feeling right now.

4. Using your lists, work with other members of your group to make a chart showing two lists of feeling words— Pleasant/Unpleasant—that were identified or used in this activity.

5. Compare your lists to the Feeling Word Vocabulary provided on the following page.

Processing the Activity:

1. How important is it to have a feeling word vocabulary in order to communicate with others?

2. Which was easier, to come up with pleasant feeling words or unpleasant feeling words? Why?

3. How are feelings related to what people do or say? Do certain feelings cause us to act in particular ways?

4. Do certain behaviors cause us to feel a particular way?

5. How would you describe the relationship between feelings and behaviors?

Notes About this Activity:

Educational Media Corporation®, Box 21311, Minneapolis, MN 55421-0311

Feeling Word Vocabulary

Unpleasant Feelings Words

Abandoned	Distraught	Left Out	Sad
Agony	Disturbed	Lonely	Scared
Ambivalent	Dominated	Longing	Shocked
Angry	Divided	Low	Skeptical
Annoyed	Dubious	Mad	Sorrowful
Anxious	Empty	Maudlin	Startled
Betrayed	Envious	Mean	Strained
Bitter	Exasperated	Melancholy	Stupid
Bored	Exhausted	Miserable	Stunned
Burdened	Fatigued	Nervous	Tenuous
Cheated	Fearful	Odd	Tense
Cold	Flustered	Overwhelmed	Threatened
Condemned	Foolish	Pain	Tired
Confused	Frantic	Panicked	Trapped
Crushed	Frustrated	Persecuted	Troubled
Defeated	Frightened	Petrified	Uneasy
Despair	Grief	Pity	Unsettled
Destructive	Guilty	Pressured	Vulnerable
Different	Intimidated	Quarrelsome	Weak
Diminished	Irritated	Rejected	Weepy
Discontented	Isolated	Remorse	Worried
Distracted	Jealous	Restless	

Pleasant Feeling Words

Adequate	Delighted	Generous	Loved
Affectionate	Determined	Glad	Peaceful
Befriended	Eager	Gratified	Pleasant
Bold	Ecstatic	Groovy	Pleased
Calm	Enchanted	Happy	Proud
Capable	Enhanced	Helpful	Refreshed
Caring	Energetic	High	Relaxed
Challenged	Enervated	Honored	Relieved
Charmed	Enjoyed	Important	Rewarded
Cheerful	Excited	Impressed	Safe
Clever	Fascinated	Infatuated	Satisfied
Comforting	Fearless	Inspired	Secure
Confident	Free	Joyful	Settled
Content	Fulfilled	Kind	Sure
		Loving	Warm

Activity 37
Finding Feeling Words

Introduction:

When learning how to respond to another's feelings, the first step is to be able to identify feeling words when they are used. Listen to what the speaker is saying. What words from the lists of pleasant and unpleasant feeling words are present? A sentence begun with "I feel" does not always mean that a feeling word follows.

With any statement, feelings may be present, but the speaker does not always express them openly. What words from the lists of pleasant and unpleasant feelings are implied in the statements where no feeling words are used?

Purpose:

- To practice identifying *pleasant* and *unpleasant* feelings words in a sentence
- To practice identifying *implied* feelings in statements

Material:

- A copy of the Feelings Exercise for each participant, pencils

Educational Media Corporation®, Box 21311, Minneapolis, MN 55421-0311

Time:

- Allow 10 minutes to complete the worksheet, plus time to process the activity

Procedure:

1. Introduce this activity with a discussion of pleasant and unpleasant feeling words. Display the Feeling Word Vocabulary (page 129).
2. Distribute a copy of the Feelings Exercise to each participant. Go over the instructions before asking them to begin.
3. After the worksheets have been completed, divide the participants into small discussion groups to process the activity.

Processing the Activity:

1. Check your individual responses with the responses of others in your discussion group. On which items did you disagree?
2. Which items did your group identify as having both pleasant and unpleasant feelings?
3. Was it easier to identify pleasant or unpleasant feelings?

Notes About this Activity:

_____

_____

_____

_____

_____

_____

_____

Feelings Exercise

Instructions:

Underline the words in the following sentences that describe either pleasant or unpleasant feelings. If no feeling word is used, write the implied feeling in the blank following the sentence.

1. It was an interesting movie. _____

2. I didn't feel the movie was very exciting. _____

3. I am afraid you will never be a football player. _____

4. If you don't practice harder, you will never make the team._____

5. Stop hitting me._____

6. Now I'm really angry. Don't hit me again. _____

7. You are so mean to me. Why? _____

8. I'm annoyed with you. Why are you such a bully? _____

9. You are too good to me. _____

10. I felt great about the victory._____

11. I enjoyed myself very much. _____

12. I'm bored. Let's go get a coke._____

13. When you tell me to quit talking, I feel you don't care about my opinions._____

14. When you don't call back, I get scared. I begin to doubt that you care about me. _____

15. I'm confused. Why did you say that? _____

16. I told you not to take me seriously. _____

Educational Media Corporation®, Box 21311, Minneapolis, MN 55421-0311

Activity 38
Listening and Responding

Introduction:

Listening is perhaps the most important skill required in working with others. A good listener communicates both interest and respect. If we are good listeners, we will avoid jumping in to direct the conversation or breaking in to make remarks that take the focus away from the person who is talking. We will avoid being preoccupied with our own thoughts. We will not let our minds wander or anticipate what the person is going to say and then jump in to complete the idea.

However, good listening is not being passive. Good listening is an active process where we are trying to understand what others are saying. We let them tell their stories in their own way. Following the lead of the talker requires both patience and practice. We will not only want to listen to the words that are being said, but we will focus on everything that is communicated, including feelings.

We encourage the other person to talk and to share more ideas and feelings when we increase our use of high facilitative responses and decrease our use of low facilitative responses. These responses are listed and summarized on the Facilitative Responses handout (page 135).

Purpose:

- To practice listening for feelings and using high facilitative responses

Materials:

- One copy of the Feeling Word Vocabulary (page 129) and one copy of the Facilitative Responses handout for each person

Time:

- 45 minutes

Procedure:

1. Distribute a copy of the Facilitative Responses handout to each participant and review the concepts with the group.
2. Divide the participants into groups of three: one speaker, one listener, and one observer.
3. The speakers should talk for 4 minutes about something that is important to them. They should choose something that is unresolved—something about which they have current feelings.
4. The listeners should take a position across from the talker, maintaining eye contact and a good listening posture.
5. The listeners should practice using feeling-focused responses, switching to other high facilitative responses when all of the feelings have been explored.
6. At the end of the four minutes, call time. Ask the observers to report on any problems or successes.
7. Rotate positions and repeat the activity twice so all of the participants in the triads can be speakers, listeners, and observers.

Processing the Activity:

1. As a speaker, how did you feel?
2. What did your listener do to *encourage* you to talk more?
3. What did your listener do, if anything, to *discourage* you from talking more?
4. What did your listener do that was most helpful?
5. As a listener, what did the speaker do that made it easy for you to listen?
6. Did your speaker do anything that made it difficult to listen?
7. Did you have any difficulty focusing on feelings at the beginning of the session?
8. What type of responses did you find difficult to refrain from making?

Educational Media Corporation®, Box 21311, Minneapolis, MN 55421-0311

Facilitative Responses

High Facilitative Responses

Feeling-Focused

Show that you are a sensitive listener by responding to the feelings that are stated or implied. Many problems and conflicts are the result of our being unaware of our feelings and how they influence behavior.

Clarifying or Summarizing

Demonstrate that you are understanding the main ideas and concepts by responding with fresh words to simplify the content of the communication.

Questions

Questions allow you to probe further into what is being said. *Closed* questions can be answered briefly, usually with a "yes" or "no." *Open* questions encourage the person to provide more expansive answers.

Facilitative Feedback as Complimenting and Confronting

Telling others how their behavior makes you feel provides needed information without judging or evaluating. Feedback can be both positive and negative.

Simple Acknowledgments

After someone has said something, it is appropriate to acknowledge that you heard it, whether you agree or disagree with what was said.

Linking

Linking people through the feelings, events, or ideas that they have in common helps to set a tone of acceptance, understanding, and mutual respect.

Low Facilitative Responses

Reassuring/Supporting

While intended to bolster the person's spirit, more often than not these responses miss their mark and the person feels misunderstood and possibly rejected. They often sense that they are being told they should not feel as they do.

Analyzing/Interpreting

While intended to explain the person's behavior and to provide some insight, these responses are filled with shoulds and oughts and conveys the message that you are superior in your approaches to situations.

Advising/Evaluating

Most people with problems really do not want advice. Evaluative remarks, even when meant as praise, are not well-received because they are judgmental and most people do not like to be judged.

Activity 39
Questioning Questions

Introduction:

Questions seems simple enough. They are designed to obtain additional information, to provoke deeper thinking, or to encourage further discussion. Although asking questions is considered to be a high facilitative response, , some types of questions are more helpful than others.

Questions can be categorized as *open* or *closed*. An *open question* encourages others to develop an answer and to talk at greater length. *Closed questions* usually call for a simple yes, no, or fill-in-the-blank type answer. Closed questions seldom encourage others to talk further which usually means we have to ask more questions. To be helpful, it would appear beneficial to the relationship to ask more open questions and fewer closed questions.

Sometimes it is best to eliminate questions entirely. Behind any question we might ask is an assumption—what are we anticipating the answer to be? If we find ourselves asking too many questions, we should try turning them into statements. Our questions now become another type of high facilitative statement—clarifying or summarizing statements.

Purpose:

- To become aware of open and closed questions
- To learn how to turn questions into statements

Materials:

- One sheet of paper and a pencil for each observer to tally the types of questions used

Time:

- 30 minutes

Procedure:

1. Review the concept of open and closed questions. Give examples of each and discuss the merits of increasing the frequency of open questions.

   Closed: *What time did you get here?*

   Open: *What happened to delay you?*

Educational Media Corporation®, Box 21311, Minneapolis, MN 55421-0311

2. Divide the group into triads. One person is to serve as the talker, one person the responder, and the third person is the observer.

3. Ask the talker to share something that is a current situation. The listener is to respond with questions. The observer is to keep track of the number of open and the number of closed questions asked. Allow three minutes for the first round.

4. Have the observers report on the questions they observed. Change roles and repeat the exercise twice.

5. Share with the group that there is an assumption behind each question. Point out that they can reduce the number of questions by turning their questions into statements.

   Example—

   Question: *How did that make you feel?*

   Statement: *It really hurt to be chosen last.*

6. Mix up the group into new triads. Have the talkers share something that is current in their lives. The responders should try to use open questions, and whenever possible, state the assumption that underlies the question as a statement.

7. The observers should tabulate the number of closed, open, and summarizing or clarifying statements used by the responder.

Processing the Activity:

1. Was it easier to formulate open or closed questions?

2. Are there any open questions that are more productive than others? (The *why* question is not as productive as *what, where, when,* and *how* questions.)

3. Did the responders seem more interested in knowing about facts or feelings?

4. What happened when you made a statement based on an assumption that was not accurate?

5. When is it best to use closed questions?

Notes About this Activity:

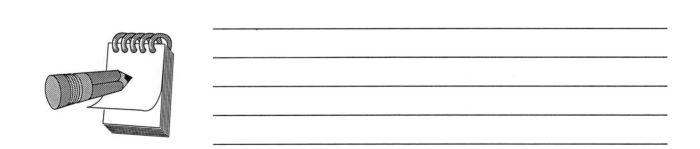

Activity 40
Trashing Pet Peeves

Introduction:

Relating with others can be frustrating. Sometimes their behavior produces a reaction of irritation, especially when we are unable to avoid interacting with these individuals.

If the unpleasant feelings persist, we may wish to consider using the negative feedback model presented in Activity 41 to let them know how their behavior is affecting us.

However, when the behavior of others is mildly annoying, we may wish simply to dismiss the behavior and to raise our level of tolerance.

Purpose:

- To reduce minor tensions caused by the mildly irritating behavior of others
- To vent unpleasant feelings before they build into major episodes

Materials:

- A pad of small note paper for each participant, pencils, bowl or hat, and a trash can or waste basket

Time:

- 20 minutes

Educational Media Corporation®, Box 21311, Minneapolis, MN 55421-0311

Procedure:

1. Remind the group that the behavior of others can sometimes be irritating, but that the incidents do not always merit providing negative feedback to others.

2. Distribute pads or small slips of paper and a pencil to each member of the group.

3. Have them list their pet peeves—behaviors of others that produce some unpleasant feelings—on individual slips of paper.

4. Fold the pieces of paper and place them in a bowl or hat.

5. Pass the bowl or hat containing the pet peeves around and ask each participant to draw one.

6. Place the trash can or waste basket in the middle of the group. Take turns sharing the pet peeves. Then crumple the pieces of paper and discard them in the waste basket or trash can.

7. Remind them that as they discard the pet peeves, they are minimizing the things that irritate them. By raising their tolerance level, they are reducing the number of potential conflicts in their lives.

8. If you wish, you can have the participants read and discard their own slips.

Processing the Activity:

1. What are some of the things that others do that irritate you?

2. Did you notice any particular pattern or theme in the pet peeves of the group members?

3. Did you experience any changes in your attitude as a result of seeing some of your pet peeves trashed?

Notes About this Activity:

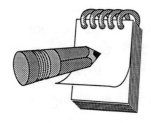

_____

_____

_____

_____

_____

_____

_____

Activity 41
Giving and Receiving Feedback

Introduction:

When we serve in roles designed to help or facilitate others, usually we keep the focus on what the other person is saying, responding to content and feelings with high facilitative responses. However, sometimes it is necessary to tell others how they affect us. When we tell others how their behavior makes *us* feel, we are giving them *feedback*. There is an art to giving—and receiving—feedback. Giving and receiving feedback can be threatening or thrilling.

The effectiveness of feedback depends on timing and readiness. It is important that we first establish a positive relationship with someone before giving feedback. Feedback is best received when the person cares about what we have to say—when we have built up some credibility by having some "chips in the bank." We begin the relationship by being a good listener, by responding to feelings, and by demonstrating that we care about the individual. If our relationship is full of honesty and respect, then our feedback will be perceived as welcome and helpful and it will strengthen the relationship.

Feedback given to individuals who are defensive will not be received—they will not respond to either positive or negative feedback.

While change is sometimes implied in feedback, those who receive the feedback are always responsible for whether or not they want to continue as they are or to change their behavior. However, if we don't know how our behavior affects others, then how can we change?

Purpose:

- To introduce the facilitative feedback model
- To experience giving and receiving positive and negative feedback

Educational Media Corporation®, Box 21311, Minneapolis, MN 55421-0311

Materials:

Time:

- A copy of the Facilitative Feedback Model for each participant

Procedure:

- 15 minutes

1. Share with the group the importance of feedback in the helping process. Stress the importance of first establishing a caring and trusting relationship before attempting to give feedback.
2. Divide the group into small groups of four to six persons. Distribute copies of the Facilitative Feedback Model handout to all participants.
3. Review the three parts to the feedback message. Remind them that the parts may be used in any order.
4. Have each person in the group select someone within the group and direct a positive feedback statement to that individual. Remind them to be specific—and positive.
5. Discuss giving negative feedback.
6. Place an empty chair in the center of each group. Ask the participants to think of someone to whom they would like to give some negative feedback. Addressing the empty chair, each participant should practice giving a negative feedback statement.

Processing the Activity:

1. What is the importance of each of the three parts to the feedback statement?
2. Which is easier to give, positive or negative feedback? Which is easier to receive?
3. How does this model differ from one where you tell the other person what to do?
4. Who retains ownership for any change of behavior required?
5. What are some things to remember before giving negative feedback? (Is the feeling persistent? Do you have a positive relationship? Choose your words carefully.)
6. How did it feel to receive positive feedback? Negative feedback?

Facilitative Feedback Model

Positive Feedback—

1. Be specific about the behavior.

Ted, yesterday when you helped me finish up my project so I could get it put away before class ended,

2. Tell how the behavior makes you feel.

I really appreciated your help

3. Tell what your feelings make you want to do.

and I would like to ask the teacher if we could be lab partners next semester.

Negative Feedback—

Timely confrontations are valuable and have a place in friendly relationships. However, you should provide negative feedback only when the other person's behavior is persistent. When giving negative feedback, make sure that you have some "chips in the bank." Build a positive relationship first so the other person will care how you are affected by the behavior. Choose your words carefully; avoid words that are loaded with emotion.

1. Be specific about the behavior.

Shawn, you promised to give my math book back today if I let you use it to study for a test. Now you tell me that you forgot it at home.

2. Tell how the behavior makes you feel.

I am disappointed when you do not keep your promises

3. Tell what your feelings make you want to do.

and I'm having trouble wanting to continue our relationship under these conditions.

Educational Media Corporation®, Box 21311, Minneapolis, MN 55421-0311

Activity 42
Sharing Feelings and Perceptions

Introduction:

When the feedback model presented in Activity 41 is used, it makes the relationship closer, no matter whether the focus is on pleasant or unpleasant feelings. Without feedback, a relationship is incomplete; there are too many blind areas. With feedback relationships can grow; communication will be more open.

When we share our feelings and perceptions of others with them, we are providing useful information concerning how they are affecting us. Sometimes the absence of positive feedback is experienced as neglect or rejection. Rejection is a very difficult emotion with which to deal because without specific feedback, the recipient is given nothing concrete on which to initiate changes.

The following should be used only in a cohesive group where mutual respect and trust have been developed.

Purpose:

- To share the feelings involved with giving, receiving, and rejection
- To provide feedback to group members about their character

Materials:

- Each participant should be told ahead of time to bring a penny, a nickel, a dime, and a quarter to the session

Time:

- Allow an average of 4 to 5 minutes per participant; best suited for small groups of 6 to 10 people

Procedure:

1. Use this activity as a closure following some type of energizer.
2. The participants should be seated in a circle on the floor.
3. Ask each person to place a penny, a nickel, a dime, and a quarter on the floor ready for use in the activity.
4. Inform the group that the purpose of this activity is to give and receive feedback within the group.
5. Tell the group that only the persons who are giving and receiving coins are to speak until the end of the activity when the activity is processed.
6. Each person is to select—from the four coins—one coin that best fits the character of a particular member of your group. When your turn comes, place the coin on the floor in front of the participant. Using some of the features of the coin (i.e., size, utility, value, inscriptions), share the reasons for selecting the particular coin to typify the person.
7. Begin with the person to your left and take turns clockwise around the circle.
8. Make the presentations speaking in the first person, maintaining eye contact with the person to whom you are presenting the coin.
9. Continue the process until all of the coins have been redistributed.

Processing the Activity:

1. Beginning with the person who has received the most coins, ask each person to share the feelings that resulted from this activity. Ask each person to direct the comments to the giver, using the first person.
2. When you get to the persons who received the fewest coins, give a brief introduction to the concept of rejection. Rejection is one of the most difficult emotional reactions with which we have to deal. Ask the participants who received the fewest coins (or none at all) to share their feelings and reactions to the exercise.
3. Was there anyone in the group who found it difficult to provide feedback? To receive feedback?
4. Was anyone influenced to give coins to someone that appeared not to be receiving any?

Educational Media Corporation®, Box 21311, Minneapolis, MN 55421-0311

Activity 43
Unraveling the Situation

Introduction:

Sometimes the situations we get tangled up in seem to be without solutions. At the onset of a problem, we might believe that there is no way out.

Even the most difficult problems have solutions. Conflicts can be resolved if we approach the situation step by step.

We must learn to work together to resolve our conflicts and to work out our problems.

Purpose:

- To demonstrate that even difficult problems have solutions
- To build a sense of togetherness within the group

Materials:

- None required

Time:

- 10 minutes

Procedure:

1. Without a great deal of preliminaries, divide the larger group into groups of 6 to 8 individuals. You can do several small groups at a time or use one group to demonstrate the concept.
2. Have those assigned to a particular group stand together in a tight circle. Separate the groups so they have room to move.
3. Tell them to reach their right hands across the circle and grasp the left hands of another member of the group. They should be holding hands with two *different* people.
4. Their task is to unravel the group without letting go of anyone's hands. The various groups can be in competition with each other to keep the activity moving or they can be timed.
5. With few exceptions the groups should be able to complete the task by working together.

Processing the Activity:

1. Did you believe it was possible to complete the task?
2. Which individuals seems to take charge of the group to coordinate movements?
3. What feelings did you experience with such close physical contact with the other members of the group?
4. What lessons did you learn about resolving conflicts and solving problems from this exercise?

Notes About this Activity:

_____

_____

_____

_____

_____

_____

_____

Educational Media Corporation®, Box 21311, Minneapolis, MN 55421-0311

Activity 44

Generating Conflict Scenarios

Introduction:

When a conflict arises between two people, sometimes there are angry words, accusations, insults, denials, and even physical violence. Strong feelings and emotions can block the search for reasonable and logical solutions.

Rather than denying these feelings, conflict resolution requires that we acknowledge the presence of these feelings in ourselves and others.

To negotiate a resolution of a conflict, both individuals must have an opportunity to state their positions. Negotiations are conducted in an atmosphere in which both agree to look at the conflict as a *win/win* proposition—to work cooperatively for a solution.

Purpose:

- To practice analyzing conflicts to determine both sides of the issue
- To suggest possible solutions to conflicts that are agreeable to both

Materials:

- One copy of the Conflict Scenarios I handout for each participant, pencils

Time:

- 30 minutes

Procedure:

1. Discuss the importance of identifying both positions when attempting to resolve a conflict.
2. Give each participant a copy of the Conflict Scenarios I handout. Ask them to identify each opposing position and to suggest a possible solution agreeable to both.
3. As an alternative, divide the group into smaller groups to discuss each scenario and to complete the assignment.

Processing the Activity:

1. Is it difficult to see both sides of a conflict when you are not involved?
2. What makes it difficult sometimes for those involved to see the other's side?
3. What might you do as a third party to get both individuals to accept a resolution to the conflict?

Notes About this Activity:

_____

_____

_____

_____

_____

_____

_____

Educational Media Corporation®, Box 21311, Minneapolis, MN 55421-0311

Conflict Scenarios I

Kevin had been going with Lisa for about two years. Their relationship started out great, but as time went on they didn't always share the same interests. Kevin would rather spend time with the guys, especially during football season. Lisa appeared to be jealous when Kevin was not with her. Kevin and Lisa had a fight one night and they agreed to break up. A couple of days later, Kevin was surprised to hear some of his friends talking about his breakup with Lisa. They knew all of the details about the fight. Some of the intimate things he had shared with Lisa were now being discussed all over the school.

Kevin's position: _____

Kevin's feelings: _____

Lisa's position: _____

Lisa's feelings: _____

Possible acceptable solutions: _____

Mr. Steinmetz has been teaching the same civics class for almost twenty years. His reputation precedes him with every new group of students. Eric did not want to take his class, but at Columbia High you don't get to choose your instructors. Eric had a straight A average going into the semester, but he knew that would not hold up. Old man Steinmetz had a reputation for not giving A's to students. It appeared that nothing you could do or say would get you an A in his class. Eric was not impressed with his first week in class. Steinmetz' lectures were so boring that he had trouble keeping awake. Then Steinmetz starting to pick on him, calling him lazy and some other things that made Eric furious.

Eric's position: _____

Eric's feelings: _____

Steinmetz' position: _____

Steinmetz' feelings: _____

Possible acceptable solutions: _____

Activity 45
Defining the Conflict

Introduction:

How you describe or define a conflict affects how you will attempt to resolve it. For successful conflict resolution, it is important to develop a skill for defining conflicts. There are several important steps to follow to define a conflict in a way that will aid in its resolution.

1. Describe the conflict in a *win/win* rather than a *win/lose* or *lose/win* fashion.

2. Don't label or judge the other person.

3. Be specific in describing the actions of the other person.

4. Describe how the other person's behavior is affecting you. How do you feel and what are you considering doing as a result of your feelings?

5. Describe what *you* could do to change *your* reaction to the situation.

It takes the cooperation of both individuals to resolve a conflict satisfactorily. Both must approach the situation with an attitude that although there is a problem, it can be solved.

Labeling, judging, or namecalling is counter productive. Anger and other unpleasant feelings must be controlled for proper communication between individuals to occur.

Don't generalize. State specifically what the other person is doing or saying that is having a negative affect on you. Generalizations and broad accusations do not provide sufficient information for the other person to know what to change.

Let others know how their behavior is affecting you. Many times things are said and done without regard to how the receiver is affected. Talk about your feelings, and what you might do as a result of your feelings.

You cannot change others. If you want a situation to change, concentrate on what you can do—how you can change your reaction to the situation.

Educational Media Corporation®, Box 21311, Minneapolis, MN 55421-0311

Purpose:

- To review the process of defining conflicts
- To focus on individual responsibilities for effecting change

Materials:

- A copy of Conflict Scenarios II for each participant, pencils

Time:

- 30 minutes

Procedure:

1. Review the material presented to introduce how we define conflicts. Emphasize the role we have as individuals in resolving conflicts.
2. Distribute copies of Conflict Scenarios II to each participant. Each person is to read the conflict and to identify the feelings resulting from the conflict. State a possible response that each individual could take to alleviate the conflict.

Processing the Activity:

1. What solution is possible for each incident that would allow both participants to win?
2. List the feelings that each person in the conflict probably experienced.
3. What would you do if you were one of the characters in each of the incidents?
4. How could an independent third person, a mediator, assist in the process of resolving these conflicts?

Notes About this Activity:

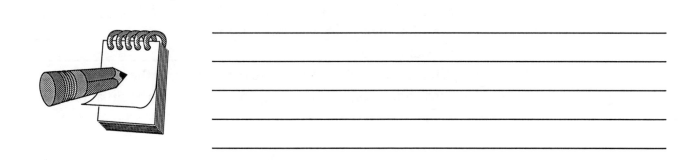

Conflict Scenarios II

Mario is Sean's younger brother, but he was born only 18 months later. Mario tries to do everything Sean does, and many times he is more successful. Mario is often given Sean's old clothes which he wears somewhat reluctantly. Last week Sean got a new jersey for his birthday. Without asking, Mario wore Sean's jersey to school, got in a fight, and the jersey got torn. Mario told Sean he would save his money and buy him a new one, but Sean said it can't be replaced.

What solution might be possible so both boys could be winners?

What labels or judgments might each have placed on the other?

Mario: _____

Sean: _____

Specifically (in your words), what did Mario do? _____

How did Mario's behavior affect Sean? _____

How did Sean *feel?* _____

What could Mario do to change his reaction to the situation?

What could Sean do to change his reaction to the situation?

Tonja never did like her name. When she was a little girl, she asked her mother why she named her Tonja. Mother just laughed and said, "I thought it was a pretty name." She never really felt that her mother understood her feelings. Tonja spent a lot of time alone in her room. She didn't have many friends and her big brother and his friends monopolized the living room and the TV.

Then this business about Tonja Harding started. Now, everyone in school seemed to know her name and there was someone teasing her every day. She was tired of being the brunt of the jokes. So, when Angie got right in her face the day that Tonja Harding entered a guilty plea in court for her role in injuring Nancy Kerrigan, Tonja gave Angie a big shove and she fell down.

What solution might be possible so both girls could be winners?

What labels or judgments might each have placed on the other?

Tonja: _____

Angie: _____

Specifically (in your words), what did Angie do? _____

How did Angie's behavior affect Tonja? _____

How did Tonja *feel?* _____

What could Angie do to change her reaction to the situation?

What could Tonja do to change her reaction to the situation?

Educational Media Corporation®, Box 21311, Minneapolis, MN 55421-0311

Activity 46

Mediating a Conflict

Introduction:

Mediation can be a quick and fair way to resolve a conflict if the persons involved agree to the participation of a mediator. Mediators are neutral third persons who are trained to lead mediation sessions. They do not take sides; they serve as impartial listeners and facilitators to help those involved come to an agreement. Mediators re-direct the energy of others from being adversaries to becoming partners, cooperating in the solution of a mutual problem.

Peer mediators are caring persons who have been trained as peer helpers. They have supplemented their training in communication and helping skills with strategies for conflict resolution and mediation.

The same *rules of confidentiality* apply to peer mediation that apply to other peer helping projects. The things that are shared in the mediation session are private—privileged communication—and they are *not* to be shared with other students.

Purpose:

- To review the basic steps of the mediation process
- To role-play a mediation session under supervision

Materials:

- A copy of Guidelines for Mediation for each participant

Time:

- 50 minutes

Procedure:

1. Distribute a copy of Guidelines for Mediation to each participant.
2. Discuss the importance of getting a commitment from both individuals involved in the dispute to agree to the stipulations for participating in mediation.
3. Divide the group into smaller groups of 5. Two individuals will role-play the opposing sides in a conflict, two will serve as mediators, and the fifth will act as an observer.
4. Brainstorm possible conflicts that might be facing students. Select one for your group to role-play.
5. Those individuals serving as mediators should keep copies of the Guidelines for Mediation before them to keep the discussion focused on the task.
6. Allow 15 minutes for the mediation session and then ask the observers to report on what they observed.
7. The mediation process is presented in greater detail (with role-play examples) in *Conflict Resolution and Mediation for Peer Helpers* (Sorenson, 1992). This book is a handbook for middle and high school students serving in the role of peer mediators.

Processing the Activity:

1. What types of conflicts were listed in the brainstorming session?
2. Which conflicts appeared to be the most interesting to role play?
3. How important is it to get those who submit their conflicts to mediation to commit to the preconditions stipulated in the Guidelines for Mediation?
4. As mediators, did you have any difficulty remembering to utilize communication skills learned in previous activities?
5. As individuals role playing the conflict, was it important to identify your feelings and to hear your position clarified by others?
6. As mediators, what would you tell others if they asked what happened during the mediation session?
7. What was the most difficult part of the process for you?

Notes About this Activity:

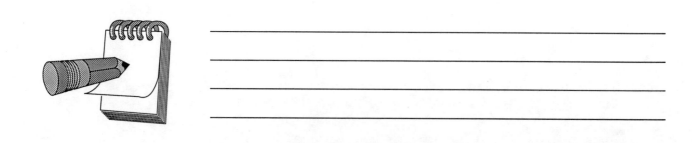

_____

_____

_____

_____

_____

Guidelines for Mediation

Before beginning mediation, the participants also should agree to:

- Commit the necessary time for the session.
- Meet in the agreed upon time and place.
- Acknowledge the responsibility and the authority of the mediator to preside over the session.
- Share their own wants, needs, feelings, and perceptions of the conflict.
- Listen to the other person's point of view without interrupting.
- Avoid labeling, judging, or blaming the other person.
- Remain calm and control their anger.
- Define the conflict as a win/win proposition.
- Brainstorm possible solutions without evaluating them prematurely.
- Commit to a solution that is agreeable to both.

The process of mediation should be orderly. Each step builds on the successful completion of the earlier steps. Here are fifteen steps that should be given attention in a viable peer mediation program.

The peer mediators should:

1. Inform others that a mediation service exists.
2. Obtain consent from those involved in the conflict to become involved in mediation.
3. Secure a safe and private location for the sharing of information.
4. Explain the need to be a good listener as the other speaks.
5. Encourage each person to tell what happened while the other listens.
6. Have each person summarize what the other person said.
7. Help both individuals identify their feelings.
8. Summarize the two positions, emphasizing the points of agreement as well as the points of contention.
9. Seek agreement from both people with the summary.
10. Ask each person to offer suggestions on how the conflict can be resolved.
11. Help the participants evaluate the choices.
12. Seek agreement for a tentative settlement.
13. Obtain a written commitment from both persons to implement the chosen solution.
14. Make arrangements to follow up this mediation session to see how the agreement is working.
15. At the request of either person, repeat the process if any person fails to live up to the agreement.

Activity 47
Planning a Day Out

Introduction:

Groups can make decisions to take action in a variety of ways. Each method has its uses and is appropriate in certain circumstances. The person with the most authority or expertise can take control and make the decisions, a vote can be taken with the majority ruling, or a group in the minority can control the group by legitimate or illegitimate means. However, the most effective method of group decision making is by consensus.

A perfect consensus would be when everyone in the group agrees to the plan of action. Getting a unanimous decision concerning a choice is difficult, but working toward consensus is an admirable goal for any group.

When the members of the group work together under conditions that are sufficiently open so that they all feel that they have a fair chance to influence the decision, then the group is working toward a consensus. When a decision is made by consensus, all the members understand the decision and are prepared to support it.

To achieve consensus, time must be allowed for the members to state their views and any opposition they may have to the views of others. They should feel that they are understood. Group members must listening carefully and respond appropriately to the feelings and ideas of others.

As this training program comes to a close, it is time to plan a group activity—something that is fun and agreeable to all.

Educational Media Corporation®, Box 21311, Minneapolis, MN 55421-0311

Purpose:

- To implement the process of decision making by consensus
- To experience a planning exercise for a practical task
- To practice listening and responding skills
- To experience the technique of brainstorming

Materials:

Time:

- One copy of Planning a Day Out for each group, pencils and paper

- Allow a minimum of 30 minutes

Procedure:

1. Review the process of brainstorming and introduce the subject of decision making by consensus. Hi-light the importance of establishing a climate where all feel free to express their ideas and feelings concerning the project.

2. Distribute a copy of Planning a Day Out to each group and read it as they follow.

   > We have come to the end of our time together as a group learning how to work together cooperatively and to reduce conflicts. Let's celebrate with a day out. We can go anywhere and do anything upon which the entire group agrees. Remember, your leader/trainer also gets to vote. Begin by brainstorming possible locations and activities. Do not censure or criticize any suggestion.

   > Next, review the list of suggestions and select the top three options. Consider the pros and cons of each suggestion. Listen to the ideas and the feelings of all of the members of the group. Take informal polls to see if any of the options are coming close to reaching consensus. Do not force anyone to agree with the majority. Listen carefully to any objections raised. Work to eliminate the objections of those in the minority by trying to meet their needs as well as those expressed by the majority.

3. Some classes have chosen to divide into smaller work units for this and other projects. Each group of 6 to 8 (with an adult chaperone/supervisor) can choose and plan their own outing.

Processing the Activity:

1. How did you feel towards certain members who did not wish to go along with the plan of the majority?
2. What were some of the suggestions made to bring all of the group members to consensus?
3. What type of leadership skills were demonstrated that brought the group together?
4. What concessions or compromises were required for the group to reach a decision?
5. Did any uncensored ideas that came out of the brainstorming session contribute to the listing of more practical alternatives? What were they?

Planning a Day Out

We have come to the end of our time together as a group learning how to work together cooperatively and to reduce conflicts. Let's celebrate with a day out. We can go anywhere and do anything upon which the entire group agrees. Remember, your leader/trainer also gets to vote. Begin by brainstorming possible locations and activities. Do not censure or criticize any suggestion.

Next, review the list of suggestions and select the top three options. Consider the pros and cons of each suggestion. Listen to the ideas and the feelings of all of the members of the group. Take informal polls to see if any of the options are coming close to reaching consensus. Do not force anyone to agree with the majority. Listen carefully to any objections raised. Work to eliminate the objections of those in the minority by trying to meet their needs as well as those expressed by the majority.

Suggestion   1 _____   2 _____   3 _____

Pros

     _____   _____   _____
     _____   _____   _____
     _____   _____   _____
     _____   _____   _____
     _____   _____   _____

Cons

     _____   _____   _____
     _____   _____   _____
     _____   _____   _____
     _____   _____   _____
     _____   _____   _____

Educational Media Corporation®, Box 21311, Minneapolis, MN 55421-0311

Selected References

Bandler, R., & Grinder, J. (1979). *Frogs into princes: Neuro linguistic programing.* Mohab, UT: Real People Press.

Community Board Program, Inc. (1992). *Starting a conflict managers program.* San Francisco, CA: Author.

Cowan, D., Palomares, S., & Schilling, D. (1992). *Teaching the skills of conflict resolution.* Spring Valley, CA: Innerchoice Publishing.

Drew, N. (1987). *Learning the skills of peacemaking.* Rolling Hills Estates, CA: Jalmar Press.

Foster, E.S. (1989). *Energizers and icebreakers for all ages and stages.* Minneapolis, MN: Educational Media Corporation.

Foster, E.S. (1992). *Tutoring: Learning by helping* (rev. ed.). Minneapolis, MN: Educational Media Corporation.

Foster-Harrison, E.S. (1994). *More energizers and icebreakers for all ages and stages.* Minneapolis, MN: Educational Media Corporation.

Hazouri, S.P., & Smith, M.F. (1991). *Peer listening in the middle school: Training activities for students.* Minneapolis, MN: Educational Media Corporation.

Hazouri, S.P., & McLaughlin, M.S. (1993). *Warm ups & wind downs: 101 activities for moving and motivating groups.* Minneapolis, MN: Educational Media Corporation.

Hazouri, S.P., & Smith, M.F. (1991). *Peer listening in the middle school: Training activities for students.* Minneapolis, MN: Educational Media Corporation.

Johnson, D.W., & Johnson, R.T. (1991). *Teaching students to be peacemakers.* Minneapolis, MN: Interaction Book Company.

Kreidler, W.J. (1984). *Creative conflict resolution.* Glenview, IL: Scott Foresman and Company.

Lankton, S. (1980). *Practical magic: A translation of basic neuro-linguistic programming into clinical psychotherapy.* Cupertino, CA: Meta Publications.

Lehr, J.B., & Martin, C. (1992). *We're all at risk: Inviting learning for everyone.* Minneapolis, MN: Educational Media Corporation.

McLaughlin, M.S., & Hazouri, S.P. (1992). *T•L•C, Tutoring•Leading•Cooperating: Training activities for elementary school students.* Minneapolis, MN: Educational Media Corporation.

McLaughlin, M.S., & Hazouri, S.P. (1994). *The race for safe schools: A staff development curriculum.* Minneapolis, MN: Educational Media Corporation.

Myrick, R.D., & Erney, T. (1978, 1984). *Caring and sharing: Becoming a peer facilitator.* Minneapolis, MN: Educational Media Corporation.

Myrick, R.D., & Erney, T. (1979, 1985). *Youth helping youth: A handbook for training peer facilitators.* Minneapolis, MN: Educational Media Corporation.

Myrick, R.D., & Folk, B.E. (1991). *Peervention: Training peer facilitators for prevention education.* Minneapolis, MN: Educational Media Corporation.

Myrick, R.D., & Folk, B.E. (1991). *The power of peervention: A manual for the trainers of peer facilitators.* Minneapolis, MN: Educational Media Corporation.

Myrick, R.D., & Sorenson, D.L. (1992). *Helping skills for middle school students.* Minneapolis, MN: Educational Media Corporation.

Myrick, R.D., & Sorenson, D.L. (1992). *Teaching helping skills to middle school students.* Minneapolis, MN: Educational Media Corporation.

Painter, C. (1989). *Friends helping friends: A manual for peer counselors.* Minneapolis, MN: Educational Media Corporation.

Painter, C. (1989). *Leading a friends helping friends peer program.* Minneapolis, MN: Educational Media Corporation.

Painter, C. (1993). *Workshop winners: Developing creative and dynamic workshops.* Minneapolis, MN: Educational Media Corporation.

Renard, S., & Sockol, K. (1993). *The collaborative process: Enhancing self-concepts through k-6 group activities.* Minneapolis, MN: Educational Media Corporation.

Sadalla, G., Henriquez, M., & Holmberg, M. (1990). *Conflict Resolution: A secondary school curriculum.* San Francisco, CA: Community Board Program, Inc.

Sadalla, G., Henriquez, M., & Holmberg, M. (1990). *Conflict Resolution: An elementary school curriculum.* San Francisco, CA: Community Board Program, Inc.

Schmidt, F. (1994). *Mediation: Getting to win win!* Miami, FL: Grace Contrino Abrams Peace Education Foundation, Inc.

Schmidt, F., & Friedman, A. (1990). *Fighting fair: Dr. Martin Luther King, Jr. for kids.* Miami, FL: Grace Contrino Abrams Peace Education Foundation, Inc.

Schmidt, F., & Friedman, A. (1991). *Creative conflict solving for kids.* Miami, FL: Grace Contrino Abrams Peace Education Foundation, Inc.

Schmidt, F., & Friedman, A. (1993). *Peace-making skills for little kids.* Miami, FL: Grace Contrino Abrams Peace Education Foundation, Inc.

Schrumpf, F., Crawford, D., & Usadel, H.C. (1991). *Peer mediation: Conflict resolution in schools* (student manual and program guide). Champaign, IL: Research Press Company.

Sorenson, D.L. (1992). *Conflict resolution and mediation for peer helpers.* Minneapolis, MN: Educational Media Corporation.

Tjosvold, D., & Johnson, D.W. (1989). *Productive conflict management.* Edina, MN: Interaction Book Company.

Webster-Doyle, T. (1990). *Tug of war: Peace through understanding conflict.* Middlebury, VT: Atrium Society Publications.

Webster-Doyle, T. (1991). *Why is everybody always picking on me?* Middlebury, VT: Atrium Society Publications.

Wenc, C.C. (1993). *Cooperation: Learning through laughter.* Minneapolis, MN: Educational Media Corporation.

Educational Media Corporation®, Box 21311, Minneapolis, MN 55421-0311